An
Activities
Handbook
for
Teachers
of
Young
Childre

Doreen J. Croft

DeAnza College

Robert D. Hess

Stanford University

HOUGHTON MIFFLIN COMPANY • BOSTON

Atlanta • Dallas • Geneva, Illinois

Hopewell, New Jersey • Palo Alto • London

An Activities Handbook for Teachers of Young Children

Second Edition

Printed in the U.S.A.
Library of Congress Catalog Card Number: 74-11945
ISBN: 0-395-19821-6

To Leta Foo

Contents

part 1   opportunities for growth in language abilities

part 2   experiences in science

part 3   exploring the arts

part 4   pre-math experiences

part 5   cooking

Introduction

If you've ever asked yourself "What am I going to do with the kids today?" this handbook is for you.

All of the activities included here come from actual classroom experience and use. They may be incorporated as central elements of the curriculum or used to supplement the program. Some are designed to provide practice in school-related skills, while others will serve to encourage creativity or simply to keep the children busy with something interesting. Most of the activities are tailored for early education programs,[1] but they can also be easily used at home or in other situations outside the classroom.

These activities are suggestions, examples and illustrations and are intended to make you more aware of the great range of possibilities for enhancing your curriculum. Try them out. Use the space on each page and at the end of each section to improve on this handbook with your own comments and notes. Revise the activities, experiment with variations, adapt them to suit your own needs. We hope they stimulate your imagination. The rest is up to you!

Acknowledgments

The authors are indebted to the following people for their direct assistance in preparing this handbook: Kay Miller, Nancy Weeks, Linda D'Addario, Marge Rose, Jean Anderson, Romayne Ponleithner, Sally Swanson, Sue Asher and Mary Ann Whiting.

We also extend special thanks to the DeAnza College and Greenmeadow student teachers, staff and preschoolers for their cooperation in planning and testing our recipes.

In addition, we have borrowed from the ideas and work of other people, and we especially wish to acknowledge the generosity of Gretchen Adams for sharing her materials on art appreciation, of Gertrude Knight for her expertise on creative dance, and of Bud Jenson for his ideas on sensorimotor explorations.

DJC
RDH

---

[1] Activities are based on principles stated in greater detail in accompanying text, *Teachers of Young Children*, Second Edition (R. D. Hess and D. J. Croft, Houghton Mifflin Company, 1975).

An Activities Handbook for Teachers of Young Children

Part 1 / Opportunities for Growth in Language Abilities

Introduction

No part of the preschool curriculum has received more attention in recent years than language development. Although our understanding of the way children learn their native tongue is incomplete, it seems certain that a rich and varied language environment helps them become more competent. These illustrations and suggestions should help the teacher provide a more stimulating and adequate language context for the child.

This part is divided into five sections: Verbalizing, Pre-writing (Visual Motor), Auditory Perception and Memory, Pre-reading (Visual Perception and Memory), and Conceptualizing. The tasks included in each of these sections were selected in order to teach children the specific skills necessary for reading, writing, discussing ideas and following instructions. Tasks with the same purpose are either grouped together or cross-referenced. They are designed to provide maximum involvement by the children, either through physical action or verbal response.

An attempt has been made to include options or variations for the teacher's use in challenging all ability levels and in providing further practice of a specific skill. These tasks can be modified for bilingual children when necessary. Make use of the space provided alongside each task and at the end of each section for your own modifications.

Dialogue has been written in most of the tasks in order to provide examples of the kinds of comments and questions which lead a child to the answers.

Materials required are often the type that the teacher can provide or make herself. The use of familiar objects is most effective in introducing a skill or concept for the first time. As the children become more knowledgeable, they can work with pictures and then abstract ideas.

The annotated list of children's books is designed to help the teacher select books for specific purposes, such as death, divorce, moving away, holidays, multi-ethnic themes and common childhood experiences. Some include suggestions for adapting to the flannel board or story telling without the book. Also useful for language motivation are picture books without words.

Language Activities

Verbalizing

#1

PURPOSE *Recognizing addresses*

Materials Flash-card for each child
Address of each child printed on the flash-card

Procedure
1. Talk about numbers on houses.
2. Talk about names of streets.
3. Mention why addresses are important.
4. Play a game:
   Read an address of one of the children and ask if anyone knows who lives there.
   Give clues, e.g., boy or girl, hair color, clothing color, etc. When child is guessed, read the address and hand the flash-card to the child who lives there.
   Follow this procedure for each child.

Variation Same procedure can be used for telephone numbers.

Suggestion Make a simple map of the city, showing streets where the children live, and let each pin a colored square on his own street.

Verbalizing

#2

PURPOSE *Learning to say names, addresses, and telephone numbers*

GAME NO. 1
Materials List of name, address, and telephone number of each child
Baseball cap
Pink satin bow (or other accessory worn by a little girl)
Policeman's hat, if available

GAME NO. 2
List used in Game No. 1
Small chair

Procedure GAME NO. 1
1. Have children form a circle.
2. Tell the children they are going to play a game about being lost.
3. Talk about how it feels to be lost.
4. Ask who might help them find their way home; ask how they could tell someone where they live; ask how they could let their parents know they were all right.
5. They may need to be guided by your saying, "Do you think a policeman could help you? How would you tell him where you live?
6. Give the various hats to the children and have them play a game about being lost.
7. It may be necessary to help the first few children by feeding them their lines.

GAME NO. 2
1. Have the children play a game of "pretend" in which they live in a magic town that has a fairy.
2. Once a year the child can ask the fairy for anything he wants; he then leaves his name and address so it can be sent to him.
3. The teacher plays the fairy and each child comes to her and tells what he wants and leaves his name and address.

> *1. Have all materials organized before starting activity.*
> *2. Limit group size.*
> *3. Plan more than one activity to reinforce each type of learning.*
> *4. Listen carefully and attentively to each child.*
> *5. Look at each child while he is speaking.*
> *6. Praise correct responses.*
> *7. Correct immediately when a child gives wrong response.*
> *8. Keep instructions simple and clear.*
> *9. Repeat instructions from time to time.*

Suggestions

1. Give children the address flash-cards used in Verbalizing #1 to look at while waiting their turn.
2. When game is finished talk about what each child wanted.
3. Cut out pictures of objects wanted and paste them on paper to make a storybook.

Verbalizing

#3

Purpose

Recognizing and describing objects

Materials

Pictures of objects mounted on cardboard (suggestions: animals, furniture, vehicles, food, play equipment)

Procedure

1. Play game called "I've Got a Secret."
2. Do not show pictures to the children.
3. Give clues about the object in the picture, e.g., physical description, group it belongs to (animal, vehicle, etc.) how it is used, where found.
4. Let children guess after each clue, e.g., "This animal has a long neck. What is it?" (giraffe)
5. When a child guesses correctly, give him the picture.
6. When all pictures are guessed, let each child hold up his picture and ask, "What is this?"
7. Encourage the children to answer in complete sentences.

Variations

1. Have children describe objects and let others guess.
2. Make animal sounds and have children guess the animal.
3. For children with limited vocabularies, use pictures of one class of objects (all food, etc.), and line pictures up to provide a visual clue.

Verbalizing

#4

Purpose

Learning to arrange in logical sequence

Materials

Manila folder or envelope for each child, with four to six squares drawn and numbered on the outside

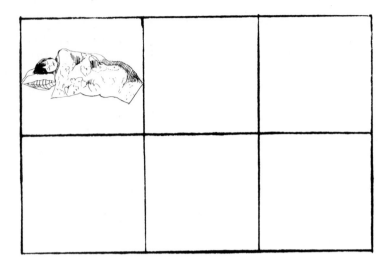

Four to six pictures showing various sequences of an activity, mounted on cardboard cut to fit the squares, inside each envelope (e.g., pictures of child in bed, getting up, dressing, eating, going to school)

First picture in sequence glued in place

Procedure
1. Using one folder as an example, show children the squares and ask what is happening in the first picture.
2. Show two other pictures and ask that they be described.
3. Put these pictures in an illogical sequence.
4. Say:
   Is that the way you do this in the morning?
   What might be a better way to put these pictures?
   Why?
5. Give each child an envelope and ask him to put the pictures in order.
6. Give help to the children who need it.
7. Talk about the pictures with each child when he finishes.

Verbalizing

#5

PURPOSE *Understanding concept of action words*

Materials Action pictures mounted on cardboard squares

Procedure
1. Hold up a picture and ask one child what is happening.
2. Say:
   Tell me about the picture.
   Who is doing the action, and is he enjoying it?
   What do you think happened before this, and what might happen next?
3. Record the child's answers, and read them back to him.
4. Repeat for each child.
5. Later display pictures along with children's answers.

HELPFUL HINTS

> 1. *Use large pictures so all children can see.*
> 2. *Hold pictures so children do not have to strain their necks.*
> 3. *Design activities to suit size of group.*
> 4. *Keep interest level up in large groups by using faster-paced activities.*

Verbalizing

#6

PURPOSE — *Forming associations between talking, writing, and reading*

Materials — Source for story information:
    photograph of child engaged in a school activity
    picture cut from magazine, catalogue, etc.
    storybook character with whom child can identify
    picture child has painted
    a tempting question, like "If you had three wishes, what would they be?"
Paper for story dictation
Construction paper for cover
Stapler

Procedure —
1. Initiate storytelling, using one of the sources listed, or take advantage of a spontaneous interest of the child.
2. Print the story as the child tells it.
3. Staple together the pictures and dictation pages.
4. Suggest the child make a cover and put name and title on it.
5. Place a "library card" in each book and let the children check them out.

Verbalizing

#7

PURPOSE — *Using complete sentences in describing an object or scene*

Materials — One each of the following objects for each child:
    red ball
    blue block
    yellow chalk
    small green ball

Procedure —
1. Hold up an object and make a statement about it:
This ball is red.
2. Ask the class to repeat the sentence as they hold up their matching objects:

TEACHER	*Is this ball red?*
CHILDREN	*Yes, this ball is red.*
TEACHER	*Is this ball blue?*
CHILDREN	*No, this ball is not blue.*

3. Introduce the other objects using the same method.
4. Introduce other objects using two qualities as a description:

TEACHER	*This ball is red and round.*
CHILDREN	*This ball is red and round.*

5. This type of language instruction calls for daily experience in patterned drill.[1]

Verbalizing

#8

PURPOSE   *Using complete sentences in describing an activity*

Materials   Group of photographs showing indoor and outdoor activities
Photographs mounted on tagboard
Sentence describing the scene below each photograph

Procedure   1. Hold up a picture and read a sentence, e.g.:
Paul is climbing the ladder.
2. Children and teacher engage in dialogue:

TEACHER	*Who is climbing the ladder?*
CHILDREN	*Paul.*
TEACHER	*What is Paul doing?*
CHILDREN	*Climbing.*
TEACHER	*What is Paul climbing?*
CHILDREN	*The ladder.*
TEACHER	*Paul is climbing the ladder. Let's say it together.* *Paul is climbing the ladder.*

Verbalizing

#9

PURPOSE   *Naming and describing single and plural objects*

Materials   Collection of cardboard or construction paper fish
Picture of a single object pasted on each fish
A paper clip attached to each fish
Small pole with string and magnet on the end

---

[1] For further suggestions on putting such a program into effect, consult Bereiter, Carl, and Engelmann, Siegfried, *Teaching Disadvantaged Children in the Preschool,* Prentice-Hall, 1966, Englewood Cliffs, N.J.

Procedure	1. Give each child a chance to fish.
	2. If he can identify the object saying, "This is a_____," he keeps the fish.
	3. Child with the most fish wins.
	4. After all the objects have been identified, children can fish again.
	5. This time they must say one other thing about the object to keep the fish, e.g., "This is a car. This car is red."
	6. When the children can easily make two simple statements, encourage them to make compound statements, e.g., "This car is red and has wheels."
Variations	1. Use objects behind a screen or partition, and a larger pole, with a clothespin on the end.
	2. If flannel objects are used, they can catch two of the same thing. Make it clear that the statement, "This is a_____" refers to one thing and the statement, "These are_____" means more than one.

Pre-writing (Visual Motor)

#1

PURPOSE	*Practicing eye movement from left to right in preparation for reading*
Materials	Mimeographed sheets with rows of dots. (Directions: make 6 heavy dots about ⅛″ thick. For first row, space dots ½″ apart across ¼ of the page. Gradually increase distance between dots with each row. Gradually lengthen the rows until they stretch across the page.)
	One large crayon for each child
	One mimeographed sheet clipped to clipboard for demonstration purposes
	Simple story book
Procedure	1. Pass out mimeographed sheets.
	2. Ask children to tell what they see on the paper.

3. Explain that dots were made one right after another; dots were made in a straight line; dots were made in row formation.
4. Review with children the above explanation.
   Ask: *What are the marks on the sheet called?*
   Say: *Put your finger on each dot (left to right).*
5. Pass out crayons and instruct children to place crayon on the first dot in the upper left hand corner. (Point at the dot on your own sheet.)
6. Have them draw lines from one dot to another, from left to right across the row (demonstrate).
7. Check each child's work and make sure he has followed directions.
8. Start other rows and remind children to draw lines from one dot to another, always beginning from left to right.
9. While they are drawing, explain to the children they are drawing lines from left to right.
10. Point to words in a book and read each sentence aloud.

Pre-writing (Visual Motor)

#2

PURPOSE

Recognizing and naming colors

Materials

Red, blue, yellow construction paper (strips ¾″ wide and 6″ long; ten strips of paper in different colors for each child)
Paste and paste brush
Containers for paste (plastic coffee lids, foil tins)

Procedure

1. Give each child strips of construction paper and pasting material.
2. Show children how to make a loop chain:
   Paste one end of a strip of construction paper.
   Bring the two ends together to form a ring.
   Thread the next strip through the first ring and paste the two ends together.
   Continue doing the same process until you have made a chain of at least eight loops.
3. Conduct an exercise in naming colors:
   Show a red strip of paper.
   Have each child find the same color strip in his group.
   Name the color and have the children repeat it.
   Select another strip of the same color and let one child name the color.
   Use the same method in teaching the other colors, blue and yellow.
4. Conduct an exercise in pattern recognition and reproduction:
   Make a model chain using three colors—repeat color pattern three times.
   Have children duplicate model chain.
   Have one child explain how pattern was put together.

Pre-writing (Visual Motor)

#3

PURPOSE   *Orienting toward right and left*

Materials   Flannel board
Felt pictures of children or animals (pictures could be cut from
    magazines and mounted on felt or sandpaper)
Pictures to represent:

zoo	trees for jungle	farm animals
circus	wild animals	barns and fences

roads or paths leading right or left (use felt strips)

Procedure   1. Place pictures of animals and children at base of flannel
    board.
2. Have children take turns choosing a picture.
3. Move pictures along paths or roads (on flannel board) in the
    direction each wishes to direct his picture.
4. Ask children which direction they are moving their pic-
    ture—right or left.
5. Encourage children to talk about what they are doing. They
    may want to tell a short story of why the child or animal is
    going to the zoo, circus, etc. Teacher may also tell a short
    story to encourage children to tell their story.

Pre-writing (Visual Motor)

#4

PURPOSE

Relating right and left

Materials

None

Procedure

1. Play the game "Follow the Leader."
2. Explain the game:
   Children are to follow what the teacher does.
   Teacher will be making turns in the directions of right or left.
   Children will be informed when the teacher changes direction.
   Children will slap the right side of their thigh when the teacher informs them that she is turning right. Children will slap the left side of their thigh when the teacher informs them she is turning left.
3. Demonstrate the game:
   Have children stand in semi-circle (children can hear and see the teacher better).
   Teacher turns her back to the children.
   Teacher turns to her right two or three times and she informs children she is turning right.
   She slaps her right thigh when she informs children she is turning right.
   She turns to her left two or three times, informing children she is turning left.
   She slaps her left thigh when she informs children she is turning left.
4. Practice the game with children:
   Have someone observe the children to make sure they understand the game.
   Select a new leader.
   Teacher can then observe children.

Variations

Different motions for the game:
Hopping to the left and right.
Taking giant steps to the right or left.
Skipping.
Jumping.
Taking a little step.

Pre-writing (Visual Motor)

#5

PURPOSE

Learning to follow a pattern and change direction

Materials

Self-sticking colored "dots" or circles
Felt tip pen, crayons, or colored pencils
Large sheet of paper

Procedure   1. Play the game "Dot to Dot":
Place a dot on the paper and ask the child to put his pen on the dot.
Place another dot a short distance away.
Have child draw a line from the first dot to the second. Be sure child keeps his pen on the last dot until the next one is placed.
Continue to place dots so the child must make lines going in different directions.
Avoid crossing lines until the child does the task easily.
Increase the length of the lines and the difficulty of pattern as the child becomes more adept.

Pre-writing (Visual Motor)

#6

PURPOSE   *Concept of a circle*[2]

Materials   Portable or wall blackboard
Oversized chalk (easier to handle)
Two or three pieces of colored chalk per child
Templates made out of $\frac{1}{8}''$ thick cardboard (use sides of boxes)

Procedure   1. Have child stand at blackboard. (Give him enough room for large circular arm movement.)
2. Begin by letting child draw anything he wishes.
3. Have him draw a large circle. If the child does not know how to do this, guide him by taking his hand and guiding his movement; encourage child to relax.
4. Trace the circle at least 6 times.
5. Use colored chalk to decorate the circle.

Variations   1. Use circle template.
2. Help child hold the template against board with the hand other than his drawing hand.
3. Have him trace inside the template, pushing against the edge of the template as he does so. Contact with the edge of the template gives child feeling of roundness.
4. Trace around six times, rest, trace around another six times.
5. Tell child templates can be used to make a design or a picture. If child wishes to make a design or a picture, give him colored chalk to do so.
6. Introduce templates of square, triangle, and diamond, in that order.

---

[2] Adapted from Kephart, Newell C. *Slow Learner in the Classroom.* Chas. E. Merrill Books, Inc., Columbus, Ohio, 1960, pp. 185–87.

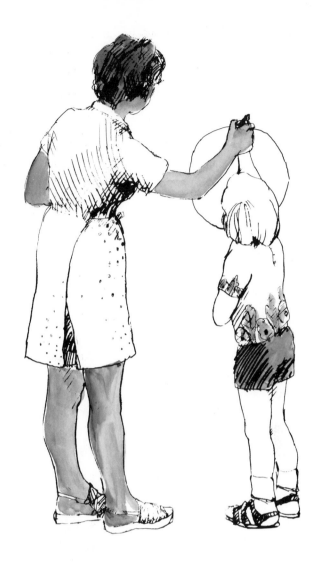

Pre-writing (Visual Motor)

#7

PURPOSE   *Concept of a square*[3]

Materials   Two or three pieces of large white and colored chalk for each
                  child
                  Blackboard
                  Eraser
                  A square template
                     Directions:
                          Use a matte knife or single-edge razor blade.
                          Cut out a piece of cardboard from the side of a box.

---

[3] Adapted from: Kephart, Newell C. *Slow Learner in the Classroom.* Chas. E.
Merrill Books, Inc., Columbus, Ohio, 1960, p. 202.

Draw a square 10″ × 10″ on the piece of cardboard.
Cut out the square.
Draw an inner square 7″ × 7″ on the 10″ square.
Cut out the inner square.

Substitute for the template:
Make an outline of a square on the blackboard. Use the side of a piece of chalk to illustrate the outline.

Procedure

1. Practice tracing squares with template on the blackboard, telling child he will be tracing a square.
2. Show him template with square; have him repeat the word "square" several times.
3. Inform child you will be helping him hold the template while he traces the square at the blackboard.
4. Have child also help hold the template with his free hand.
5. Tell child to push gently against the edge of the cardboard while tracing the square. Teacher can help by guiding the child's hand movements.
6. Trace square six times. Help child count the number of times he has traced the square.
7. After a short rest, the child may like to resume tracing.
8. Make sure child is making *pointed corners* instead of rounded ones.
9. Use colored chalk to decorate squares.

Pre-writing (Visual Motor)

#8

PURPOSE

Printing first and last names using upper and lower case letters

Materials

Clear plastic folder for each child
Name of child printed on a piece of paper and inserted into each folder
Felt pen or crayon for each child
Paper towel or sponge for wiping off ink or crayon on folder
Alternate materials which can be used:
piece of cardboard with name of child printed on it
crayon

Procedure

1. Give each child a folder with his name printed on it.
2. Read his name to him.
3. Tell children they will be printing their own names.
4. Explain to children how to use their materials:
Tell children their name is printed on a piece of paper and inserted inside the plastic cover.
Use felt pen to trace over letters on the plastic cover.
Wipe printing off with paper towel or sponge.
5. Instructions for printing letters:
Start by printing the big letters.
Do one letter at a time.
Begin with the big letters on the left working toward the right.

HELPFUL HINTS

> 1. *Make mental note of children who do not participate.*
> 2. *Plan activities for individual children or small groups of children who are reluctant to speak up in a large group.*
> 3. *If you are yelling a lot, it's time to stop and reassess your method of presentation.*
> 4. *Sometimes it helps to start an activity with a finger play or short song, then introduce the learning activity when you have everyone's attention.*
> 5. *Give instructions before showing the items.*
> 6. *Keep in mind the sequence of activities so you can make a quick transition from one to another. (Hesitate and you're lost!)*

Observe children to make sure they are printing each letter from left to right.
6. Give children a chance to ask questions.

Variations
1. This same technique can be used to allow children to copy shapes. Start with the circle and progress to square, rectangle, triangle, and diamond.
2. This technique can be used to teach children to print letters of the alphabet. Start with lower case letters one at a time.

Auditory Perception and Memory

#1

PURPOSE
Recognizing sounds

Materials
Bag or box with lid
Noisemaking objects, e.g., bell, rattle, whistle, paper (to tear), pieces of sandpaper (to rub together), cricket, horn

Procedure
1. Say:
We are going to play a listening game.
When we are listening what do we hear? Noises. Every day we hear lots of noises.
What do we hear the noises with? Ears.
Take your hand and wiggle your earlobes, like this.
I have a box with some things in it that make noises. I am going to make a sound and then ask who can tell me what is used to make that sound.
Cover your eyes with your hands.
2. Make a sound with one of the objects and ask who knows what object made the sound.
3. Go through the entire selection of objects, trying to call on each child.
4. When the children become more adept at identifying the sounds, have them cover their eyes while you make two sounds. Ask if the sounds were the same.

5. After this first introduction, the children can play this in a group by taking turns being the one who chooses the noise-makers.

Auditory Perception and Memory

#2

PURPOSE *Hearing and repeating sound sequences*

Materials Noisemaking objects: bell, rattle, sandpaper, paper (to tear), wooden blocks (to hit together)

Procedure
1. Start with three objects on the table.
2. Hold up one object and ask if anyone knows what it is called and what it does.
3. Pass it around and let each child use it. Do the same with the other two objects.
4. Say:
   I am going to make three noises. First I will shake this rattle, then I will ring the bell, and last I will tear the paper.
   What noise did you hear first?
   What noise did you hear next?
   What noise did you hear last?
5. Give another example.
6. Ask the children to cover their eyes with their hands.
7. Have them listen carefully to more noises and then have them make the same noise.
8. Add new objects and increase the number used.
9. Introduce sounds they can make (clapping, stamping, tongue clicking).

Auditory Perception and Memory

#3

PURPOSE *Practicing beginning-sounds of words*

Materials Shoe boxes
Variety of toys which children can easily identify

Procedure
1. Print one letter of the alphabet (in upper and lower case) on the end of each shoe box. Next to the letter draw or paste a picture of a common object which begins with that letter. Place five or six objects beginning with that letter in each box.
2. Place one shoe box on a table.
3. Let children examine and name objects in the box.
4. Pass the box around to a small group of children and let each child take one object.

5. Ask each child to name what he has.
6. When a child responds, reinforce by repeating the name of the object, e.g., "Bob has a bat."
7. Have the group repeat the name of each object and collect each object as it is named.
8. If a child cannot name his object, say:
   Mary, show everyone your object. Can anyone name it?
9. After all objects are collected, hold each one up and ask:
   What is this?
   Did you hear anything special about the names of these things?
   Who can tell me the name of the letter on the shoe box?
10. Bring out a second shoe box with a different letter on it. Repeat above procedure.
11. Mix all the objects from both boxes.
12. Let each child pick one object, name it and replace it in the appropriate shoe box. Continue in varying degrees of difficulty according to children's abilities.

Auditory Perception and Memory

#4

PURPOSE *Identifying and grouping objects beginning with the same sound*

Materials Sources for pictures: color books, catalogues, magazines
Scissors
Crayons
Paste
Box for storage (on outside of box, print upper and lower case letters and paste picture of object—see Auditory Perception and Memory #3)

Procedure   1. Show the children the box with the identifying letter and picture.
2. Ask:
   Who can tell me the name of this letter?
   What is this? (picture)
   This box is for pictures of things that begin with the B sound such as bicycle—can you say bicycle?
3. Pass out the picture books and ask the children to show you when they have found a picture beginning with the same sound as bicycle; have them identify the object and say the word bicycle for comparison.
4. If correct, the child can color it or cut it out and paste it on a card.
5. Repeat this activity with all of the consonants.
6. After two or three cards have been collected, they can be used by individual children for sorting into beginning-sound groups, or used to play "Which One Doesn't Belong" (display three cards with the same letter, one with a different letter).
7. It is helpful to place a strip of paper over the letters at the top of the cards so that the only clues are the sound similarities or differences.

Auditory Perception and Memory

#5

PURPOSE   *Hearing rhyming sounds and matching rhyming objects*

Materials   Box, approximately 6″ × 9″ with lid
Collection of small toy objects with rhyming names (e.g., tire, wire, hook, book, shell, bell, fork, cork, cane, plane, mouse, house)
Construction paper "mat" (6″ × 9″) marked off into 6 sections of 3″ × 3″

Procedure   1. Give a child the box (filled with the small toy objects) and ask him to take everything out of it.
2. Ask if he can tell you the name of each object.
3. If he cannot name each object, help by asking:
   Is it a—?
4. If the child still does not know, name the object for him and have him repeat after you:
   This is a—.
5. Follow the same procedure with all the objects, naming each.
6. Ask the child if the names of any two of these things sound the same.
7. If he seems confused, line up three objects, two that rhyme and one that doesn't. Have him name these three objects, and ask him again which ones rhyme.
8. When he hears the rhyming sounds and can find matching

items, he can put each pair in a square on the construction paper mat.

Auditory Perception and Memory

#6

PURPOSE — *Identifying familiar sounds*

Materials — Tape recorder and microphone

Procedure —
1. In preparation for the class experience, tape some common sounds of activity, for example:
   In the kitchen: getting things out of the cupboard and placing them on the counter, using the egg beater, frying bacon, or anything that sizzles, washing dishes
   In the bathroom: brushing teeth, washing hands, flushing the toilet, taking a bath or shower
   In the yard: running the sprinkler (hearing the rhythm of it hitting the sidewalk), pruning a hedge, edging the grass, running the lawnmower, raking leaves
   At the market: sound of the door opening, the cart being pulled apart from the others, cans being piled on one another, opening the chiller door to get milk, hearing the paper bag being popped open, and the cash register ringing
2. Ask the children to listen closely and see if they can tell where the person was when he recorded the sounds and what was happening.
3. Encourage them to remember as many different sounds as they can.
4. Play the tape again and ask what sound they heard first.
5. Play three sounds, stop the tape and ask which sound was first, what was next, and what last. Increase the number of sounds heard as children are successful.
6. After doing this activity once, the children might have some ideas as to what they would like recorded.

Auditory Perception and Memory

#7

PURPOSE   *Recognizing right and left hands*

Materials   Simple, home-made picture book showing:
    top of left hand with fingers and thumb spread,
      the word "left" printed beneath it
    top of right hand with fingers and thumb spread,
      the word "right" printed beneath it
    left hand, palm up
    right hand, palm up
    left and right hand on same page, palms down
    left hand and right hand, one palm up, one down
    same as above, reversing positions
(Trace your own hands to make the pictures or use the hands of a child)

Procedure   1. Say:
    This is a book about hands. That word on the cover says "hands."
    There are pictures in the book of hands. See if you can make your hands look like the pictures.
    Here is a picture of a left hand. Can you make one of your hands look like this?
    Put your hand on the table below the picture in the book. Are your fingernails showing?
    Do your thumb and finger next to it make a shape that looks like an "L"?
    Is your thumb in by your stomach or out by your shoulder?
  2. Repeat for top of right hand.
  3. For palm up, ask:
    Are your fingernails showing? Do you see lines on the hands?
    Is your thumb nearest your stomach or your shoulder?
  4. When using a picture of two hands, help the child to get one hand positioned first, then the other.
  5. If child copies hand positions right away, talk about how he did it.

Auditory Perception and Memory

#8

PURPOSE   *Following directions*

Materials   Noise-making objects: bell, rattle, two wooden blocks, eggbeater
Other objects: book, chair, ball, baseball cap

Procedure   1. Say:
    This game we are going to play is about careful listening. See this bell? What can you do with it?

See that chair? What can you do with it?
I am going to ask you all to listen carefully while I tell you what to do.
Then I will ask who wants to do it.
First shake the rattle, then put on the baseball cap. Who wants to do that?

2. Continue, giving only two directions until the group seems to find that easy.
3. Then give three tasks in a row.

Variations

1. The teacher can select one child and ask him to do two tasks. Then let him choose someone else, etc.
2. Ask which child would like to get four items. If the school has a store, then the game could be about grocery shopping.
3. Teacher can move around the room touching three or four children or objects. She can then ask who can remember who or what was touched. If a child has difficulty, hints can be given as to hair color, clothes worn, or for object, its shape, color, etc.
4. When children are outside, give directions such as, take two big steps, hop, turn around, etc.

Auditory Perception and Memory

#9

PURPOSE

Following the sequence of action in a story[4]

Materials

A book which includes a conflict, real or unreal, and expresses negative as well as positive feelings and actions

Recommended Books: Brown, Margaret W., *The Runaway Bunny,* New York: Harper and Row, 1942; Brown, Margaret W., *The Dead Bird,* New York: Wm. R. Scott, 1958; Zolotow, Charlotte, *The Quarreling Book,* New York: Harper and Row, 1963; Rey, H. A., *Curious George,* Boston: Houghton Mifflin Co., 1941.

Procedure

1. Read in an interesting manner. Read intimate passages softly, exciting passages more forcefully; read slowly for suspense and faster for action.
2. Check to discover if the children understand the following:
   Words. If a word is not familiar to the children, e.g., being "lost," "curious," "sad," "friendly," then ask if they know what the word means. If the action in the story explains the word, ask how the story explains it and discuss it.
   Abstract concepts. If a book is about an abstract concept, e.g., fast, soft, round, secret, mystery, ask if anyone knows what

[4] Adapted from Stern, Virginia, "The Story Reader as Teacher," *Young Children,* XXII:1, October, 1966, pp. 31–43.

the key word means. Encourage them to give examples or descriptions and look for what the story tells them about that word.

Character motivations. Ask why the boy is sad, how they know he is sad, and what they think would make him happy. Pictures and words in the book can be used as clues.

Processes. Ask why something happened, what will happen next, what could the subject of the story do to solve his problem in another way.

3. Encourage children to participate by accepting their answers and expanding them. If necessary, clarify meanings. Show them their thoughts are important and interesting to you.

Pre-reading (Visual Perception and Memory)

#1

PURPOSE   *Recognizing different shapes, colors, and patterns*

Materials   Three squares for each child (10″ × 10″ made from construction paper of the same color; center of each square marked with an X, designating area for paste)

Paste and brush

Containers for paste (plastic coffee can lids or tin foil pans)

For use by groups of four children:

Three-sectioned TV dinner foil trays filled with the following three groups of items cut from construction paper: yellow circles, 3″ diameter; red squares, 3″ diameter; green triangles, 3″ to a side

For teacher's demonstration purposes:

Decorate two large blue squares with two yellow circles

Decorate one large blue square with one small red square

Procedure   1. Show children the squares, circles, and triangles.
2. Have children repeat the names of the shapes.
3. Note the color of each shape.
4. Have children repeat both the color and the shape.
5. Give each child three blue squares with an X in the center, and pasting materials.
6. Have each child choose one square or one circle or one triangle from the TV dinner foil tray.
7. Have him glue this to the blue square.
8. Stop activity, and demonstrate matching and non-matching patterns:
(Have children hold squares.)
Show them similar patterns—two blue squares decorated with two yellow squares. Ask if they are alike.
Introduce another blue square—decorated with a smaller red square.
Ask children if the patterns are now all alike.
Ask which squares have the same shapes glued on them.
Ask which squares are different.

9. Have children choose two more shapes from the TV tray, one like the first one they chose, and one that is different.
10. Proceed with the activity by decorating the blue squares with different shapes. (The object of the activity is to have two matching shapes pasted on two different blue squares and one non-matching shape pasted on a blue square.)
11. Gather the squares as the children finish. Squares can be backed with sandpaper and used on the flannel board for discussion purposes. The teacher can discuss why certain members in a group are alike and why some members are not alike.

Pre-reading (Visual Perception and Memory)

#2

PURPOSE   *Matching identical symbols*

Materials   Hand-made Christmas ornaments (can be made from construction paper)
Suggestions for ornaments:
A pair of candy canes
A pair of angels
A pair of Christmas trees

Pairs of different shaped ornaments, (round, square, triangle, etc.)

Pictures of Christmas themes cut from catalogue and reinforced by construction paper backing

Paste and brush

Containers for paste (foil pans or milk bottle lids)

Felt tree pinned to wall

Straight pins on tips of branches or wherever possible on the felt tree

Hole-puncher and strings

Alternatives:

Live tree and real ornaments

Procedure

1. Have children glue matching pictures or ornaments on to matching shaped paper ornaments.
2. Punch hole at the top of each ornament and string.
3. Give each child one ornament from a set.
4. Hang the other half of the ornament on the felt tree where straight pins have been placed.
5. Have each child find the matching ornament on the felt tree and hang it beside the mate.
6. Have children go in pairs.

Pre-reading (Visual Perception and Memory)

#3

PURPOSE   *Recognizing differences in objects*

Materials   Strips of cardboard 4″ × 20″ (on which have been drawn four identical objects and one which is different)

Examples:

Four squares and one circle

Four balls and one bat

Four triangles and a fifth upside down

Four F's and one facing backward

Four cups with spoons, one cup without a spoon

Four B's and one D

Four hats with feathers, one without a feather

Procedure

1. Start with objects with obvious differences, proceeding to the less obvious. Place the different object in different places, so child doesn't use position as a clue.
2. Say:
   I have some cards with pictures on them.
   On each card all the shapes will be the same except one.
   I would like you to see if you can find the one that is different and tell why it is different.
3. Help children observe the differences in shape, e.g., that squares have four sides and pointed corners and the circle has no corners.
4. Allow children to trace shapes with their fingers to help them understand the different shapes.

AN ACTIVITIES HANDBOOK FOR TEACHERS OF YOUNG CHILDREN

Pre-reading (Visual Perception and Memory)

#4

PURPOSE
Recalling members of a group of objects by color

Materials
Plastic spoons of different colors

Procedure
1. Show the children four spoons of four different colors.
2. Review the colors.
3. Say:
   I am going to hide one of the spoons and you can take turns telling me which one is missing.
4. Encourage children to answer in complete sentences, e.g., "You are hiding the red spoon."
5. When child guesses correctly he may hold the spoon.
6. Children can play this game with one another, once they have learned it.

Pre-reading (Visual Perception and Memory)

#5

PURPOSE
Recalling members of a group of objects

Materials
A collection of four to seven objects: e.g., toy boat, plastic cup, ball, book, orange, small stuffed animal, toy car, whistle
Some different kinds of fruit

Procedure
1. Line up the first group of objects.
2. Ask children to name the objects.
3. Ask children to cover their eyes while you take away two objects.
4. Ask who can tell what was taken away.
5. Follow up with the same game using the fruit.
6. After playing awhile, ask if it was easier to remember which of the fruit was missing or which object was missing.

Pre-reading (Visual Perception and Memory)

#6

PURPOSE
Remembering what one sees

Materials
Five objects, each 4″ tall
Example: a doll, a hat, a box of crackers, a cup, and a book (opened and standing)
Alternative: Use cardboard shirtboards, folded in half so they will stand up. On each side of the shirtboard, paint a different letter of the alphabet, using the same color paint

Procedure   1. Start with only three objects, increasing to four, then five, as children become more acquainted with them.
2. Ask children to name the objects and tell something about each one, e.g.:
The doll has black hair and a red dress.
3. Play a game:
Have children cover their eyes with their hands.
Place objects in a row.
Have children uncover their eyes and look at the objects, starting from left to right.
Have them look at the objects to see which one comes first, second, third, etc.
Choose one of the children to come up, turn away from the objects, and name them in order starting from left to right.
If child names the objects in the proper order, he may change the arrangement and choose the next child to do the naming.

Pre-reading (Visual Perception and Memory)

#7

PURPOSE   *Recognizing patterns*

Materials   White glue or paste
Triangles, cut from 2″ square pieces of construction paper
Cardboard strips, 2″ × 8″
Sample cards with different triangular designs, four triangles to a card

Procedure   1. Hand out pasting material, four triangles, and a cardboard strip.
2. Show children the sample cards with different triangular designs.
3. Ask children what they see on the cardboard strips.

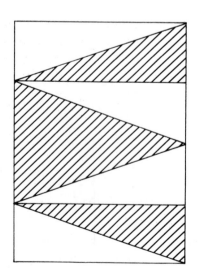 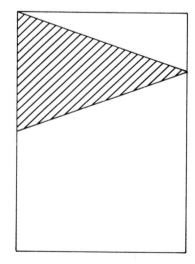

4. Ask if they know what shape is used in the design.
5. Ask:
    Where would I put my first triangle if I wanted to make a design just like the sample card? (Put it in the wrong corner and let children tell where it should be placed.)
    Where would I put my second triangle?
6. Give each child a sample cardboard strip.
7. Have them make a design duplicating the one on their sample.
8. Help when necessary, but do not actually place triangle for them. Help them decide which corner the triangle goes into, or if the shapes are touching, etc.
9. Say:
    When you have finished, I will come and see what you have done. Then you may glue your pieces on and take the design home with you.

Pre-reading (Visual Perception and Memory)

#8

PURPOSE

Sorting objects according to shape

Materials

A deep cigar box or shoe box
Two construction paper mats on which to place sorted objects
Round objects, e.g., beads, buttons, thumb tacks, spools, bottle caps, pebbles, marbles, fake money, corks, small paper plates or toy dishes
Square objects, e.g., bolts, empty matchbooks, sugar cubes, dice, individual ice cube molds, erasers
Alternatives: Round buttons and square buttons, red buttons and white buttons (or any two colors), two-holed buttons and four-holed buttons

Procedure

1. Sit down with child and take an object out of the box.
2. Ask child to name the object. (Encourage child to reply in a complete sentence.)
3. Have child take each object out, one at a time.
4. Have child tell what each object is.
5. When he is finished, put two round objects and one square object on the table.
6. Ask:
    Is there anything the same about these objects?
    Is one different? How?
7. Encourage child to feel the roundness or squareness of the objects.
8. Put all the objects back in the box.
9. Put down the two paper mats.
10. Have child put all the same shapes in one pile and other shapes in another pile.

Variation

Provide a box full of objects which can be sorted according to size, shape, and color.

Specify criteria such as "round" or "red," etc. and have the children take turns selecting an object which fits the criteria.

Pre-reading (Visual Perception and Memory)

#9

PURPOSE   *Sorting objects according to size and/or color*

Materials   Red and white buttons (include large and small of each color as well as buttons with different numbers of holes)
Cigar box or shoe box
Two small boxes for sorting or two paper mats

Procedure

1. Ask child to find what is in one of the boxes.
2. Say:
   Can you tell me about this object? (Give him a large red button.)
3. Encourage child to name the button, describe the shape, color, and the number of holes it has.
4. Give him time to think about what he wants to say.
5. If necessary, direct him by asking:
   If a button was missing from your coat and you needed a new one just like this one, how could you tell what it looks like?
6. Compare a red button with a white one to encourage him to see the color difference.
7. Compare the number of holes in the buttons.

Supplementary learning

1. Ask child to sort buttons in any manner he wishes, putting the buttons in as many piles as he thinks necessary.
2. Then ask him to put the buttons into two piles, using the mats or small boxes. If he sorts the red ones from the white ones ask him if he can put the buttons together in another way, i.e., small and large or two holes and four holes, etc.

Pre-reading (Visual Perception and Memory)

#10

PURPOSE   *Learning directional words: in, out, up, down, across, through, into*

Materials   Playground equipment or substitutes:
Big cement pipe (sewer pipe—3 feet in diameter) or wooden barrel, steel drum or large cardboard box (use for crawling *through,* going *into*)
Slide (climbing *up* and sliding *down,* or a kitchen chair-stool)
Six inch wide board, four to five feet long, supported on either end by wooden boxes, bricks, etc. (Walking *across*)
A wagon or large box (sitting *in* and getting *out* of)
Camera to take pictures of children doing the actions

HELPFUL HINTS

1. *Use language to help children focus on their activities: "Johnny uses both hands to hold on"; "Mary is hopping on her right foot"; "Peter knows how to go down the slide slowly. Now he's going very, very slowly."*
2. *Make comments that encourage responses: "I wonder how you made this design." "That's an interesting way to do it." "I'd like to have you tell me more."*
3. *Phrase comments and questions that require more than a "yes" or "no" answer. Instead of "Do you want to read a story?" you might say, "I wonder if you remember the fun story we read yesterday about the silly bear."*
4. *Squat or kneel down to the child's eye level when you talk with him.*
5. *Get into the habit of putting your arm around a child or making some kind of physical contact when you communicate verbally.*
6. *Be conscious of the way you stand and sit. Your posture invites or rejects physical contact from others.*

Procedure

1. Play "Follow the Leader."
2. Explain that the leader has to tell what he is doing and the others copy his actions and words.
3. First time through, help the children to know what words to use by asking the leader to do something. That is, "Show us how you go up."
4. As children do various activities, have someone take pictures to be used for a discussion at a later date.

Supplementary learning

1. Show the pictures to the children.
2. Write down the conversation that takes place when they discuss the pictures.
3. Using the pictures and the dictation, make a book, underlining the action word.

Pre-reading (Visual Perception and Memory)

#11

PURPOSE

Learning relational concepts: behind, on top, inside, outside, in front, beside

Materials

Three boxes covered with colorful paper
   small box with a top
   middle-sized box
   large box
Three stuffed animals or dolls

Procedure

1. Place boxes in a row.
2. Ask children to identify what you have and how many there are.
3. Talk about the parts of a box (sides, bottom, top).
4. Ask how they could use boxes (for keeping things, toys, presents, small parts of games, etc.).
5. Put each doll with one box and tell the children you are going to talk about where each doll is.
6. Put one doll on top, one behind, and one inside.
7. Ask:
   Where is this doll? (Point to doll on top of small box.)
8. Continue with the other dolls.
9. Review the questions and answers.
10. Put a doll beside the box and ask where she is.
11. Place the next doll in front of the box and proceed with questioning.
12. Review the last two positions.
13. Put a doll underneath a table or chair and talk about that.
14. Let children put the doll in a place and tell where they put it. Then ask them to put the doll on top of, behind, under, etc.
15. Play "Simon Says," using a box for each child.

HELPFUL HINTS

> *1. Cut heavy construction paper or good quality scrap paper into flash cards approximately 3″ × 6″.*
> *2. Have each child think up a word he would like to have for his own.*
> *3. Print each word with felt pen in large neat letters.*
> *4. Give the words to the children and encourage them to keep a collection to share with the class and their families.*

Pre-reading (Visual Perception and Memory)

#12

PURPOSE   *Learning names of letters*

Materials   A magnetized board with two sets of lower case letters and upper case letters (or a flannel board with two sets of lower and upper case letters)

Procedure
1. Place four lower case letters in the column on the left-hand side of the board.
2. Place identical letters on the right-hand side of the board, making certain that no two identical letters are opposite each other.
3. Point to the first letter in the left-hand column and ask if anyone knows what the letter is called.
4. When it has been identified, ask if anyone can show you a letter in the second column which looks the same.
5. When a matching letter has been identified, pick it up and place it beside its mate in the left-hand column for close comparison.
6. Match remaining letters in the same way.
7. Repeat several times, encouraging different children to respond.
8. Do this with all the lower case letters, and then work through the alphabet using the upper and lower case together.
9. Then work with only the upper case letters to be sure the children associate the symbol with its name.

Pre-reading (Visual Perception and Memory)

#13

PURPOSE   *Matching identical letters*

Materials   One cardboard square per child, divided into nine small squares with a different letter of the alphabet printed in each square
Plastic or cardboard letters of the alphabet
Box or tin can with deep sides (three pound coffee can) to hold letters

> *1. Praise correct responses.*
> *2. Tell children when they are wrong. Give the correct response, have the child repeat it, and follow this with praise.*
> *3. Do not say the child is wrong, but that his response is wrong. "No, that letter is B," rather than "You're wrong, Charles. That letter is B."*
> *4. Stop a teaching activity while children are still motivated and interested.*

Procedure

1. Give each child a card.
2. Explain that there are letters of the alphabet on each card.
3. Say:
   In the can are letters of the alphabet. Some of these will match the ones on your card.
4. Have the children take turns drawing the letters out of the can.
5. As each one draws, ask if he knows the name of the letter.
6. Ask him to repeat the name as he looks at the letter.
7. Ask if he can find it on his card.
8. Give help when needed.
9. If there is no match, child puts the letter back in the can.
10. Next child takes a turn.
11. The first child to fill in a row across or down wins the game.

Pre-reading (Visual Perception and Memory)

#14

PURPOSE

Recognizing printed names

Materials

A manila envelope for each child upon which he has drawn his own face

A rectangular piece of tagboard for each child, with his first name written in upper and lower case letters

Those cardboard letters needed to make his name

Piece of flannel board or bulletin board for demonstrating

Procedure

1. Place name-card and letters inside each envelope.
2. Print child's name in upper left-hand corner of the envelope.
3. Pin a name card on the flannelboard.
4. Pin the required letters at random on the board.
5. Say:
   Remember when you drew your face on an envelope?
   I am going to show you some things you can keep in your envelope.
   On the board is a card with the name "Mike" on it.
   Here are some letters which can be used to make the name "Mike."

We will start here, on the left-hand side and work to the right. Who can find the big "M" and place it under the one just like it on the card?
(Point to "M" on card.)

6. Continue to complete name.
7. Mix up the letters and let several children make the name.
8. Give each child his envelope.
9. Tell them they may each make their own name and that you will help when needed.
10. Later each child can learn his last name in the same manner.

Supplementary learning   When a child can copy his name easily, show him the card and ask him to make his name from memory.

Conceptualizing

#1

PURPOSE   *Identifying and classifying foods*

Materials   Samples of one of the following classes of foods:
Fruits (apples, oranges, grapefruit, apricots, plums, prunes, figs, tangerines, bananas, avocados, tomatoes, cherries, etc.)
Vegetables (peas, green beans, carrots, turnips, celery, collard greens, pea pods, radishes, lettuce, green peppers, squash, etc.)
Meats (pictures of different cuts of meat or ways of serving, examples of precooked meat [weiners, beef jerky, lunch meat] etc.)
Grains (cereals, breads, rice, noodles, macaroni, crackers, etc.)
Dairy Products (cheeses, milk, ice cream, butter, eggs, etc.)

Procedure
1. Consider explaining this project to the parents and asking them about some of the foods served frequently in the home.
2. Parents might be willing to prepare one dish for the child to bring to school.
3. Discuss with the children the kinds of things they eat at home to provide a base for classification.
4. If you start with fruit, for example, bring 5 common varieties.
5. Talk about color, shape, and texture of skin.
6. Hold up an apple and ask if anyone can tell what it is.
7. Hold up an orange and have it identified.
8. Introduce three more.
9. Cut open the fruit and show the children what it looks like inside.
10. Call attention to the seeds and the fact that all fruit contains seeds.
11. Cut fruit into sections and give to each child to taste.
12. Talk about taste (sour, sweet) and whether pulp is crisp or hard or soft or juicy.

1. Children like teachers to share in a learning experience.
2. Join in on activities and laugh with the children.
3. Let children draw your outline while you lie down on a large piece of butcher paper.

13. Talk about ways we can use fruit (pies, jams, dried, juices, etc.).
14. Follow up with tasting experiences of processed fruit.
15. Consider field trip to a grocery store.

Supplementary learning

After learning some of the different kinds of food, set up a store, using wooden boxes, benches, or bookcases. Ask children to bring in empty food boxes, cartons, meat trays, and cans from home. Children can make *papier maché* fruit, meat, etc., and paint them with tempera or cover them with pictures mounted on cardboard. Let the children sort the items and put them into groups of fruit, vegetables, etc. Help them make signs and then let them play store.

Conceptualizing

#2

PURPOSE

Learning parts of the body, left and right side

Materials

Large roll of butcher paper
Large black crayon
Tempera paints
Scissors

Procedure

1. Conduct a discussion about parts of the body. Say:
   Can anyone tell me what the word "body" means?
   Does John have a body, does Lisa, do I?
   What are some of the parts of our bodies?
   Do we all have arms? (Hold arms in air and shake them).
   We all have arms; what else do we all have?
2. After some discussion, show children the paper, crayon, and paint.
3. Explain that they will lie on the paper and you will trace around them. Then they can cut out the shapes and paint them; after that they can put in a face and draw the clothes. Encourage naming and discussion of body parts.
4. When tracing around the child, start at the head, saying:
   I am starting at the top of your head.
5. Mention the body parts as you trace, stressing right and left sides.
6. The figures can be hung on the walls with name cards under them.

Supplementary learning	1. Play "Simon Says." Use directions as "pat your head, shake your left leg, wriggle your right-hand fingers," etc.
	2. Make a puzzle. Draw a figure of a boy and a girl. Mount it on cardboard. Cut the cardboard into parts of the body.
	3. Act out and sing "Put Your Finger in the Air."

Conceptualizing

#3

PURPOSE	*Learning concepts of shape (round and square)*
Materials	Round objects such as ball, bottle cap, marble, can, plastic drinking glass, pencil
	Square objects such as block, pad of paper, eraser, book
Procedure	1. Put round objects on a table.
	2. Ask children to name the objects.
	3. Ask if anyone knows what the word "round" means.
	4. Hold the ball up and say:
	The ball is round.
	Trace around it with your fingers.
	5. Have the children trace a circle in the air.
	6. Pass the other objects around and let children find the roundness of the objects and trace around them.
	7. Place a block or other square object on the table and ask:
	Is this round?
	How do you know this isn't round?

> 1. *Teach concepts over and over again in different areas of the school; incorporate them into other parts of the curriculum.*
> 2. *Remind children of the concepts they learned earlier.*
> 3. *Have them demonstrate what they learned.*
> 4. *Review and repeat learned concepts frequently.*

8. Help children talk about the differences by asking:
   Do round things have corners? Do round things have sides? What shape is this? This is square.
   What do you think will happen if we try to roll this block? What will happen if we roll the ball?
9. Pass the square things around and let the children trace them.

Conceptualizing[5]

#4

PURPOSE *Learning concepts of hard and soft*

Materials Hard objects such as block, thick plastic, wood, rock, spoon
Soft objects such as cotton ball, sponge, pillow, marshmallow

Procedure 1. Let children handle the hard objects.
2. Discuss things that are hard.
3. Ask if their heads are hard or soft; if their stomachs are hard or soft, etc.
4. Provide a soft object for contrast.
5. Let children handle soft objects.
6. Discuss soft things they know about.
7. Have children look around the room for hard and soft objects.

Conceptualizing

#5

PURPOSE *Learning concepts of light and dark*

Materials Light colored objects such as piece of pastel material, picture of a sunny scene, toy or stuffed animal which is light colored
Dark objects such as piece of dark colored cloth, picture of dark cloudy scene, toy or stuffed animal which is dark colored

Procedure 1. Let children handle and look at the light colored objects.

---

[5] Conceptual activities No. 4–9 deal with relational concepts and not absolute qualities. The teacher can emphasize comparison in the form of "harder than," "softer than," "longer than," "faster than," etc.

2. Discuss light colored things.
3. Ask questions about their clothing, their hair, their skin.
4. Ask what happens if the shades are pulled, or if the lights are shut off. Demonstrate.
5. Provide contrasting objects so children can see and talk about the opposite concept.

Conceptualizing

#6

PURPOSE

Learning concepts of hot and cold

Materials

Hot water bottle filled with hot water
Bowl of ice cubes

Procedure

1. Pass the hot water bottle around.
2. Ask how it feels.
3. Ask:
   Who can think of something we eat or drink that is hot?
4. Pass the bowl of ice cubes around.
5. Ask how it feels.
6. Ask:
   Who can think of something we eat or drink that is cold?
   How do you feel when the weather is hot; when it is cold?

Conceptualizing

#7

PURPOSE

Learning concepts of fast and slow

Materials

Pictures of things that go fast such as airplane, speedboat, racing car, bus, train
Pictures of things that go slow such as baby crawling, turtle, snail, worm, old person with a cane

Procedure

1. Introduce pictures of things that go fast.
2. Talk about why people use them.
3. Introduce contrasting pictures.
4. Talk about why some things are slow.
5. Find things in the classroom that go slow or fast.

Conceptualizing

#8

PURPOSE

Learning concepts of large and small

Materials

Large cardboard box or block
Very small cardboard box or block

Procedure
1. Let children see the large box.
2. Let them crawl inside it and explore it.
3. Talk about the concept of large and have them name things they think are large.
4. Show them the small box and let them hold it.
5. Talk about the things they think are small.

Conceptualizing

#9

PURPOSE   *Learning concepts of loud and soft*

Materials   At least one of the following: drum, wood blocks, or party horn

Procedure
1. Say something to the children in a soft voice and ask if you were speaking in a loud or soft voice.
2. Say something loudly and ask how you were talking.
3. Ask them to say something softly.
4. Ask them to say something loudly.
5. Discuss when we need to use loud voices and when we need to use soft voices.
6. Talk about how important it is to speak in a loud voice when we have to warn someone of danger, yell for help, call a dog, show we are angry.
7. Talk about times when we speak in a soft voice, such as when someone is sleeping and we do not wish to disturb them, or when we are at the hospital or library, sometimes when we are in school, or when we have a secret.
8. Use wood blocks or drum or party horn to demonstrate loud and soft. Let children practice making loud and soft sounds with instruments.

Conceptual Games

PURPOSE   *Classifying and analyzing the quality of objects*

GAME NO. 1—MATCHING
Materials   Pictures pasted in two rows on cardboard, covered with construction paper (protect with clear contact paper)
Examples of objects that might be included in pictures: face, tree, apple, wheel, wagon, plate with food, leaf, eye

Procedure
1. Insert shoestring (knotted underneath at one end) next to each picture on the left hand side.
2. Punch holes next to each picture on the right hand side.
3. Have children connect pairs of objects that can be conceptually matched, by inserting shoestring in the proper hole (e.g., face–eye).

GAME NO. 2—SORTING
Materials   Large manila folder, outside divided into two sets of squares

1. Browse in bookstores; go to book sales.
2. Ask local librarian about library book sales.
3. Start a collection of favorite books for yourself.
4. Write your own "custom designed" story just for your class.

Pictures of two different categories of things contained in folder
Examples of categories:

fruits	flying things
animals	vegetables
wheeled things	plants
objects of same color	objects of same shape

Procedure
1. Have children divide pictures into two categories and place each picture in one of the squares marked on the outside of the envelope.

GAME NO. 3—CLASSIFYING

Materials
Flannelboard and shapes of animals commonly owned by children (each category of animal, e.g., dogs, cats, guinea pigs, should be the same shape and color)

Procedure
1. Ask children:
   Who owns a dog?
2. Count the number of children who own a dog and place the appropriate number of dog shapes on the flannelboard.
3. Repeat the same procedure with each animal.
4. After figures are placed on the board, ask:
   How many animals do you children have? Let's count them. How many are dogs? (Count)
5. Do the same with all the other animals. Be sure to also stress those which DO NOT belong to a category.
6. As children become more sophisticated, add other categories, such as clothing, food, color of hair and skin, and types of transportation.

Bibliography of Resources

The following list of books includes all-time favorites of teachers who have relied on story books to dramatize an event, to quiet a group of children, to extend the child's experiences, to excite and enliven the imagination, to teach specific concepts, and to amuse, delight, and involve children in the joys and beauty of the written and spoken word. These story books are all suitable for the preschool child. The categories were selected to help the teacher find books to meet special needs. Some are annotated with suggestions for adapting to flannel boards or memorizing for storytelling; others are better for reading with one child on your lap, still others for dramatizing with a group. The teacher will find many other helpful resources in the library and bookstores. Each person will develop his or her own favorite list of books depending on his or her likes and dislikes. Other sources of book lists and pamphlets are listed at the end of the bibliography.

All-Time Favorites

Anglund, Joan Walsh. *A friend is someone who likes you.* New York: Harcourt, Brace & World, 1958.

——. *Love is a special way of feeling.* New York: Harcourt, Brace & World, 1960. Both of these books are excellent to look at, read, and talk about with one child. They are small, easy to hold and delightfully illustrated; topics are geared to the experiences of the young child.

Austin, Margot. *Barney's adventure.* New York: E. P. Dutton, 1941. A favorite for telling without a book and showing the pictures afterwards or adapting to the flannel board. Barney is a little boy who wants to see the circus, but has no money for a ticket. On his way home he sees large tracks and follows them into the woods hoping to capture and return one of the circus animals in exchange for a ticket. Instead he finds a clown who gets him into the circus after all.

Bannon, Laura. *The scary thing.* Boston: Houghton Mifflin, 1956. A boy and his farm animal friends are frightened by some scary eyes and noises. It is dark, lumpy-like, and hides in the bushes. The scary thing turns out to be a newborn calf.

Barrett, Judi. *Animals should definitely not wear clothing.* New York: Atheneum, 1971. Illustrates how uncomfortable it would be for certain animals to wear clothing. Clear bright graphics by Ron Barrett showing how silly each animal would look wearing hats, sweaters, and other clothes. Funny to children. Good for discussion.

Bonne, Rose, and Alan Mills. *I know an old lady.* Chicago: Rand McNally, 1961. This is an illustrated version of the favorite folk song by Alan Mills, "*I know an old lady who swallowed a fly.*" The teacher can cut out flannel pictures or outlines of the characters and use them for telling or singing the tale with the flannel board. Music included at end of the book.

Borten, Helen. *Do you move as I move?* London: Abelard-Schuman, 1963. The text calls attention to the various kinds of movement all around us. The child can see movement as "lazy as a yawn" or flowing movements "that ooze as smoothly as honey," and other common experiences which challenge him to think about and try movements. This is one of a series including *Do you see what I see?* and *Do you hear what I hear?*

Brooke, Leslie (illus.). *The three bears.* London: Frederick Warne. This is the classic tale which never fails to delight youngsters. Good for telling without the book and then showing pictures. Also good for teaching concepts of big and small, hot and cold, hard and soft, etc.

Brown, Margaret Wise. *Goodnight moon.* New York: Harper & Row, 1947. This is an old standby of a bunny in bed who says goodnight to the moon, stars, and noises until he falls asleep.

Brown, Margaret Wise. *The runaway bunny.* New York: Harper & Row. A bunny tells his mother he is going to run away, but his mother tells him she will find him because he is her little bunny. A pretend story told and illustrated in a gentle tender way.

——. *The noisy book.* New York: Harper & Row, 1939. This is a good story for young children about the noises a little dog named Muffin hears as he walks around the city. The children enjoy participating in guessing about and making the noises.

——. *The indoor noisy book.* New York: Harper & Row, 1942. Another book about Muffin the dog which encourages children to participate and guess about the noises indoors. The teacher can use this for telling without a book.

Burton, Virginia Lee. *The little house.* Boston: Houghton Mifflin, 1942. A Caldecott medal winner about a little house in the country that eventually becomes surrounded by urban development and the happy ending when it is jacked up and moved back to the country again.

Charlip, Remy. *Mother, Mother, I feel sick. Send for the doctor, quick, quick, quick.* New York: Parents' Magazine Press, 1966. A child has a stomach ache and the doctor finds all kinds of hilarious things in his stomach from a plateful of spaghetti to a two wheeled bike. This funny story can be adapted for the flannel board or presented as a shadow play behind a sheet.

Craig, M. Jean. *The dragon in the clock box.* New York: W. W. Norton, 1962. Joshua seals an empty clock box and tells his family there is a dragon's egg in it. No one gets to see it except Joshua. A delightfully imaginative tale.

Cutler, Ivor. *Meal one.* New York: Franklin Watts, 1971. Helbert wakes up one day with a plum in his mouth. He and his mum decide to plant it under his bed, and exciting things happen. Imaginatively humorous illustrations by Helen Oxenbury.

Daughtery, James. *Andy and the lion.* New York: Viking, 1938. Andy removes a thorn from a lion's paw and the grateful lion helps to make Andy a hero.

De Regniers, Beatrice Schenk. *May I bring a friend?* New York: Atheneum, 1964. When the King and Queen invite the hero of the story to tea he asks to bring a friend. His friend turns out to be an animal. He is invited to lunch, dinner, breakfast, Halloween, etc. and each time he brings different kinds of animals until the King and Queen finally go with him to the zoo. The teacher can adapt this to the flannel board by using cut-outs of crowns to represent the King and Queen and simple silhouettes or magazine pictures of zoo animals with sandpaper backing.

_____. *Something special.* New York: Harcourt, Brace, & World, 1958. A book of poems with titles such as "A Sugar Lump is Good to Have in Case of," and "What's the Funniest Thing?" This is an all-time favorite for children and their parents and teachers.

Dines, Glen. *The useful dragon of Sam Ling Toy.* New York: Macmillan, 1956. Sam Ling Toy finds a lizard which he takes back to his shop in Chinatown. His friends the children help him care for it until it grows up to be a dragon. The friendly dragon causes much confusion and distress until he finds a useful place in leading the Chinese New Year's parade.

DiNoto, Andrea. *The star thief.* New York: Macmillan, 1967. A storyteller's delight about a thief who steals all the stars from the sky and nails them into barrels for safekeeping. The story theme is easy to learn without memorizing every word. Show the pictures after telling the story.

Emberley, Barbara. *Drummer Hoff.* Englewood Cliffs, N.J.: Prentice-Hall, 1967. An adaptation of a folk tale, brightly illustrated, in rhyme about all the soldiers who help to build a cannon, but Drummer Hoff "fired it off" in a colorful blast at the end. Trace the figures to adapt to the flannel board. Repetitive rhyme is fun to recite.

Ets, Marie Hall. *Play with me.* New York: Viking, 1955. A little girl goes out to the meadow to play, but the animals are frightened of her. When she sits quietly they gradually come out to "play."

Ets, Marie Hall. *Talking without words.* (*I can, can you?*) New York: Viking, 1968. Animals can make their wishes known without words. The book calls attention to the many ways we can communicate without words. Look for other titles by this well-known author.

Flack, Marjorie. *Ask Mr. Bear.* New York: Macmillan, 1932. This is an old favorite about a little boy who doesn't know what to give his mother for her birthday so he asks a series of animals who make suggestions which he rejects until he finally asks Mr. Bear, who gives him a wonderful solution. Good for adaptation to flannel board. Also easy to tell without the book.

_____. *Wait for William.* Boston: Houghton Mifflin, 1935. An old favorite about a little boy who was left behind by his older brother and sister on their way to see a circus parade because he had to stop to tie his shoe. Later, he has no trouble getting the older children to wait for him, after they have seen him riding on the elephant in the parade and want to hear him tell how he got such favored treatment.

Freeman, Don. *Corduroy.* New York: Viking, 1968. A little girl falls in love with a teddy bear no one else wants. Look for other books by this popular author.

Gag, Wanda. *Millions of cats.* New York: Coward-McCann, 1928. This is an old classic which is familiar to many who tell and enjoy Wanda Gag's stories. It is about an old man and an old lady who collect so many cats that they end up with "hundreds of cats, thousands of cats, millions and billions and trillions of cats." Fun to read and an easy story to tell without the book. Show the pictures after telling the story.

Green, Mary McBurney. *Is it hard? Is it easy?* New York: Young Scott Books, 1960. Silhouette type photographs of children doing such things as skipping, tying shoes, catching a ball, doing a somersault, etc. Encourages sharing and discussion of individual skills.

Harper, Wilhelmina. *The gunniwolf.* New York: E. P. Dutton, 1946. This is a suspenseful and humorous tale about a little girl who wanders too far into the woods to gather flowers and is accosted by the gunniwolf. Excellent story for telling without the book. Show pictures afterward.

Hitte, Kathryn. *Boy, was I mad!* New York: Parents' Magazine Press, 1969. A little boy is so mad he decides to run away from home, but he sees so many interesting things when he goes out that he forgets he is running away.

Hobart, Lois. *What is a whispery secret?* New York: Parents' Magazine Press, 1968. A delicately illustrated book about quiet things like leaves whispering in the breeze and kittens and frogs making soft sounds, and holding someone close and whispering "I love you." A good lap book.

Holdsworth, William Curtis (illus.). *The gingerbread boy.* New York: Farrar, Straus and Giroux, An Ariel Book, 1968. The classic story about the gingerbread boy who runs away from the little old woman and the little old man and the cow and the horse, etc., until he meets up with the sly old fox. Good for telling without the book or can be easily adapted for the flannel board.

Ipcar, Dahlow Zorach. *The marvelous merry-go-round.* New York: Doubleday, 1970. Appealing story of the circus with good woodblock illustrations.

Kantor, MacKinley. *Angleworms on toast.* New York: G. P. Putnam's

Sons, 1969. This is a humorous story, delightfully illustrated by Kurt Wiese, about a boy who requested angleworms on toast whenever he was asked what he wanted to eat. This made everyone sick! Finally they got even with him by serving him just what he wanted.

Keats, Ezra Jack. *Over in the meadow.* New York: Four Winds Press, 1971. A familiar counting rhyme about the activities of meadow animals and their young. Beautifully illustrated by this well-known artist. Useful for flannel board counting.

Krasilovsky, Phyllis. *The man who didn't wash his dishes.* New York: Doubleday, 1950. This is an amusing story about a man who was always too tired to do his dishes after dinner so he let them pile up until he finally had to eat out of his ash trays, soap dish, and flower pots. He finally piles all his dirty dishes into his truck, sprinkles soap on them, and drives around on a rainy day.

_____. *The very little girl.* New York: Doubleday, 1953. The story about a very little girl and how small she was in comparison with the big chair, a kitchen stool, a rose bush, etc., until she realizes one day that she is bigger than all these objects. Can be adapted for the flannel board to show relative size.

Krauss, Ruth. *The bundle book.* New York: Harper & Brothers, 1951. Children identify easily with the strange bundle under the blankets which moves and puzzles mother who tries to guess what it is.

_____. *The growing story.* New York: Harper & Brothers, 1947. A little boy watches the animals and plants around him grow, but his arms and legs look the same to him until he tries on some of his old clothes and discovers he has grown too.

Leydenfrost, Robert. *The snake that sneezed!* New York: G. P. Putnam's Sons, 1970. Harold is a snake who leaves his forest home to make his way in the world. Good for adapting to flannel board use.

Lifton, Betty Jean. *One legged ghost.* New York: Atheneum, 1968. Japanese folk tale about a boy who finds an umbrella and doesn't know what it is. Show the lovely pictures after you tell the story so as not to give away the suspense.

Lionni, Leo. *Inch by inch.* New York: Ivan Obolensky, 1960. An inchworm uses his ingenuity to stay alive by measuring different birds, but a nightingale decides to eat him.

Lowery, Lawrence F. *Sounds are high, sounds are low.* New York: Holt, Rinehart and Winston, 1969. Sounds can be different and this rhyming book calls attention to the sounds which are familiar to a young child.

Marsh, Corinna. *Flippy's flashlight.* New York: E. P. Dutton, 1959. A little boy discovers how a flashlight can help him find all his lost toys.

Mayer, Mercer. *There's a nightmare in my closet.* New York: Dial Press, 1968. A child has nightmares about monsters in his closet until he finally decides to invite them into bed with him.

McCloskey, Robert. *Blueberries for Sal.* New York: Viking, 1948. This is a standard book for most preschool children about a little girl who goes out with her mother to pick blueberries, and a little bear who goes with his mother to eat blueberries. The babies get mixed up to the surprise of both mothers. McCloskey's story and illustrations are excellent. Other titles by this author are highly recommended (*One morning in Maine; Make way for ducklings*).

Nash, Ogden. *Custard the dragon.* Boston: Little, Brown, 1959. An imaginary tale in rhyme about a cowardly dragon named Custard. Every child should be familiar with Ogden Nash's humorous story.

Phoebe. *Noses are for roses.* New York: McGraw-Hill, 1960. "Arms are for hugging, tugging, lugging, slugging." "Fingers are for tickling, patting, tapping, snapping," etc. Different parts of the body can do different things.

Potter, Beatrix. *The tale of Peter Rabbit.* Grand Rapids, Mich.: The Fideler Company, 1946. Children love this classic tale of Peter Rabbit and his adventures in Mr. McGregor's garden. Good for telling without the book. Show pictures later.

Rice, Inez. *The March wind.* New York: Lothrop, Lee & Shepard, 1957. This is a fantasy about the exciting things that happen to a little boy when he wears the hat belonging to the March wind.

Rogers, Joe (illus.). *The house that Jack built.* New York: Lothrop, Lee & Shepard, 1968. This is the simple Mother Goose tale which is repetitive and is excellent for use on the flannel board. These illustrations can be traced onto pellon or flannel.

Schurr, Catherine. *Cats have kittens—do gloves have mittens?* New York: Alfred A. Knopf, 1962. Children enjoy participating in this humorous book about animals interspersed with questions similar to the title of the book. .

Sendak, Maurice. *In the night kitchen.* New York: Harper & Row, 1970. A highly imaginative story about a child's dream of falling into cake batter and bread dough. A good story to tell with dramatic gestures. Be sure to show the imaginative illustrations.

———. *Where the wild things are.* New York: Harper & Row, 1963. This a fantasy about a little boy named Max who is sent to his room for misbehaving and he imagines that he sails away to a place where the wild things are. Illustrations are highly imaginative. Some teachers like this book very much and others think the pictures are frightening. Winner of the Caldecott medal.

Shaw, Charles G. *It looked like spilt milk.* New York: Harper & Row, 1947. Some large white shapes look like all kinds of things but turn out to be clouds in the sky. This is excellent for flannel board use. Trace the shapes onto pellon and let the children answer "no" as each shape is named and placed on the flannel board.

Schulevitz, Uri. *Rain, rain rivers.* New York: Farrar, Straus & Giroux, 1969. A girl listens to the rain outside her window and imagines it falling on places near and far away. She thinks about her friends and how they will play in the puddles. Lovely "rainy-day" type illustrations.

———. *One Monday morning.* New York: Charles Scribner's Sons, 1967. A boy in a city tenement dreams of royalty coming to visit him. A good story to adapt to the flannel board to teach days of the week.

Skorpen, Liesel Moak (Emily McCully, illus.). *That mean man.* New York: Harper & Row, 1968. A delightful story about a mean man and his family who did "mean" things like crayoning on the walls, spilling their cocoa, slopping their soup, and other things that young children can easily identify with.

Slobodkin, Louis. *Moon Blossom and the golden penny.* New York: Vanguard Press, 1963. A poor child in Hong Kong receives a lucky penny when she helps an old woman. Pictures are small. Tell the story and let children look at the illustrations in small groups. Fun to give each child a gold covered chocolate "coin" when the story is over.

Slobodkina, Esphyr. *Caps for sale, a tale of a peddler, some monkeys & their monkey business.* New York: William R. Scott, 1947. This is one of the all-time favorites of teachers and children. Easy to tell without the book, children always love to hear this story about a peddler trying to sell the colored caps which he carries around on top of his head.

Steadman, Ralph. *Jelly book.* New York: Stroll Press, 1970. Charming illustrations and a humorous story about the very "complicated" process of making jello gelatin.

Steig, William. *Sylvester and the magic pebble.* New York: Simon & Schuster, 1969. Sylvester is a donkey who loves pebbles. He finds a magic pebble and turns into a big rock. Ends with a happy family reunion. Caldecott award winner. This story is good for telling, even though there is a lot of text.

Stobbs, William. *Henny-Penny.* Chicago: Follett, 1969. Here is another classic for telling with the flannel board. Repetitive tale about Henny-Penny who says the "sky's-a-going to fall!".

Ungerer, Tomi. *Crictor.* New York: Harper & Brothers, 1958. This is a story about the imaginative antics of a snake named Crictor who is the friend of a French lady, Madame Bodot.

_____. *Zeralda's ogre.* New York: Harper & Row, 1967. A suspenseful tale about an ogre who loved to eat children, especially for breakfast, until Zeralda teaches him to like her exotic cooking. Large colorful illustrations. Fun to tell.

Viorst, Judith. *I'll fix Anthony.* New York: Harper & Row, 1969. Younger children can relate to this humorously written story about little brother who is planning all kinds of revenge on big brother Anthony.

Waber, Bernard. *"You look ridiculous," said the rhinoceros to the hippopotamus.* Boston: Houghton Mifflin, 1966. An amusing story in which a hippopotamous learns to appreciate what he looks like. Fun to tell without the book.

Weil, Lisl. *Fat Ernest.* New York: Parents' Magazine Press, 1973. The tale of what happens when a preschooler and his two pet gerbils move into a big housing project with an unfriendly neighbor across the hall.

Welber, Robert. *The winter picnic.* New York: Pantheon Books, 1970. Adam wants to go on a picnic, but it is snowing outside, and his mother feels that it might be better to postpone the picnic until summer. Mother is too busy to play with him, but Adam finally convinces her to go out, and she discovers that he has fashioned plates, cups, and bowls out of snow. Warm feelings of sharing and encouraging a child's imagination and ingenuity.

Wither, Carl. *The tale of a black cat.* New York: Holt, Rinehart & Winston, 1966. This well-known drawing story is one which the author (narrator) illustrates as the story unfolds. He creates line drawings to accompany each episode. Encourages storytellers to invent and illustrate their own creations.

Zion, Gene. *Harry the dirty dog.* New York: Harper & Brothers, 1956. A dog named Harry hides his bath brush and proceeds to get very dirty. His family no longer recognizes him when he tries to convince them he is Harry. He finally retrieves his brush and is happy to be bathed.

Zolotow, Charlotte. *Sleepy book.* New York: Lothrop, Lee & Shepard, 1958. Interesting descriptions of how birds and beasts settle down for the night. Ends with children tucked in their beds.

1. Make a book from children's art, and have them help write a story about their pictures.

2. Tape-record stories about children's dreams.

3. Start a story and have the children finish telling it.

4. Cut out magazine pictures and have children tell stories about them.

5. Make a book of children's art along with their comments to send home to sick children or to use as thank-you notes to special visitors, like the dentist, doctor, and other community volunteers.

6. Make the reading area more inviting with a rug, pillows, rocking chair, and table lamp.

Books of Poetry and Nursery Rhymes

Chalmers, Audrey. *I had a penny.* New York: Viking, 1944. A story in rhyme about a child who walks to the store to spend her penny. Very good for telling without a book. Teacher can hold a penny in her hand and use this story as a basis for discussion about money and what it buys. Also good for teaching safety.

Ciardi, John. *You know who.* Philadelphia: J. B. Lippincott, 1964. A book of poems about children who pout, hide, misbehave, and are mischievous. Titles include "Someone Showed Me the Right Way to Run Away," "Get up or You'll Be Late For School, Silly!"

deAngeli, Marguerite. *Book of nursery and Mother Goose Rhymes.* Garden City, N.Y.: Doubleday, 1955. Large, colorfully illustrated book with index of first lines and familiar titles.

Field, Eugene. *Wynken, blynken and nod.* New York: Hastings House, 1964. Barbara Cooney's "dream-like" illustrations capture the mood of this classic children's poem.

Fisher, Aileen. *In the woods, in the meadow, in the sky.* New York: Charles Scribner's Sons, 1965. Poetry relating to title of book.

Frank, Josette. *Poems to read to the very young.* New York: Random House, 1961. A selection of poems about common events and topics of interest to the preschool age child.

Kuskin, Karl. *In the middle of the trees.* New York: Harper & Row, 1958. Poetry good for use with one child or small group.

Livingston, Myra Cohn. *Listen, children, listen: an anthology of poems for the very young.* New York: Harcourt, Brace, & Jovanovich, 1972. An excellent collection for any program of early education. Illustrations by Trina Schart Hyman.

Lord, John Vernon. *The giant jam sandwich.* Boston: Houghton Mifflin, 1973. "One hot summer in Itching Down, Four million wasps flew into town." Imaginatively detailed illustrations by John Lord and verses by Janet Burroway tell a delightful story of how a town cooperates to rid themselves of wasps with a giant jam sandwich. Encourage children to look at and talk about all the details.

Merriam, Eva. *Catch a little rhyme.* New York: Atheneum, 1966. Delightful, popular book of rhymes.

Milne, A. A. *Now we are six.* New York: E. P. Dutton, 1955. Every child should be familiar with A. A. Milne. See also *When we were very young.*

Petersham, Maud. *The rooster crows.* New York: Macmillan, 1955. Caldecott award winner. Rhymes, skipping games, and fingerplays.

Prelutcky, Jack. *Lazy bird and other verses.* New York: Macmillan, 1966. Catchy verses designed to accompany childlike illustrations by Janosch.

Raskin, Ellen. *Who, said Sue, said whoo?* New York: Atheneum, 1973. "The cross-eyed owl said whoo, The polka dot cow said moo; Then who, said Sue, said chitter-chitter-chatter, and titter-tatter, too?" That's the question woven into a nonsense rhyme in which more and more silly animals climb aboard Sue's car until they find the answer to her question.

Reed, Philip (illus.). *Mother Goose and nursery rhymes.* New York: Atheneum, 1964. Illustrated in woodcuts printed in six colors. Selections are excellent and the art is worth discussing with the young child.

Stevenson, Robert Louis. *A child's garden of verses.* New York: Franklin Watts, 1966. A classic combining poetry with storytelling. Illustrated by Brian Wildsmith.

Tenggren (illus.). *Mother Goose.* Boston.: Little, Brown, 1960. One of the more popular Mother Goose books for the preschool.

Updike, John. *A child's calendar.* New York: Alfred A. Knopf, 1966. Book of poetry.

Wells, Rosemary. *Noisy Nora.* New York: Dial Press, 1973. "Jack had dinner early, Father played with Kate, Jack needed burping, So Nora had to wait. . . ." Being the middle child in a family means having to wait and wait, so Nora gets into all kinds of mischief and finally decides to run away. The story of a family of mice in simple verse portraying familiar childhood experiences.

Wildsmith, Brian (illus.). *Mother Goose.* New York: Franklin Watts, 1964. Well illustrated and colorful.

Multi-Ethnic Books

Baker, Betty (Arnold Lobel, illus.). *Little runner of the longhouse.* New York: Harper & Row, 1962. Little Runner is envious of his older brothers who are allowed to participate in the Iroquois New Year's ceremonies. Young children will be able to identify with his persistence in trying to convince his mother that he is not too young. He finally persuades her to give him a bowl of maple sugar.

Baker, Bettye F. *What is black?* New York: Franklin Watts, 1969. Imaginative text and photographs explain how "Black is sometimes a color. At other times it is an idea."

Bond, Jean Carey. *Brown is a beautiful color.* New York: Franklin Watts, 1969. A story in simple rhyme calling attention to all the things around us that are brown.

Cannon, Calvin. *Kirt's new house.* New York: Coward, McCann & Geohegan, 1972. The excitement of helping to build a new house is shared by a black child and his family in Macon County, Alabama, through the Self-Help Housing Program. Photographs by Elaine Wickens. See also *What I like to do,* by the same authors, about the life of a seven-year-old and the warmth of his family in Alabama.

Clark, Ann Nolan. *In my mother's house.* New York: Viking, 1941. A book of simple verses describing the Pueblo Indian—the land, the people, their homes and animals. Velino Herrera's stylized illustrations depict the Pueblo lifestyle.

Ets, Marie Hall. *Gilberto and the wind.* New York: Viking, 1963. A little Mexican boy finds in the wind a temperamental playmate—one who can fly kites, capture balloons, scatter leaves, run races. The wind can be a stormy and quiet companion. Charming pencil sketches.

————. and Aurora Labastida. *Nine days to Christmas.* New York: Viking, 1959. A story about Ceci, a five-year-old Mexican girl who selects her piñata for Christmas. Illustrations and text give the child a picture of how Christmas is spent by children in modern day Mexico. The story may be a bit long for reading to a large group of very young children but it lends itself to sharing with a small group who can talk about and look at the pictures.

Flack, Marjorie, and Kurt Wiese. *The story about Ping.* New York: Viking, 1933. An old favorite about a little duck who lives on a boat on the Yangtze River and his adventures when he hides from his master in order to avoid getting a spank on the back. Children identify easily with not wanting to get a spanking.

Greenberg, Polly. *Oh lord, I wish I was a buzzard.* New York: Macmillan, 1968. A black girl goes to work in the cottonfield "with the sun shining pretty on the land." Before the day's end, she has imagined changing places with a buzzard, a butterfly, a dog, and other creatures. Written in a simple, rhythmic style, with bright, warm illustrations.

Keats, Ezra Jack. *Goggles!* Toronto: Macmillan, Collier-Macmillan Canada, Ltd., 1969. Two black children find a pair of motorcycle goggles but have to outsmart a gang of "big guys" in order to keep them. The author is well known for his excellent stories and illustrations and in this book he "tells it like it is" for a little boy in the big city.

Keats, Ezra Jack, and Pat Cherr. *My dog is lost!* New York: Thomas Y. Crowell, 1960. Juanito, who speaks only Spanish, has just arrived in New York from Puerto Rico and is sad because he lost his dog. His search takes him to Park Avenue, Chinatown, and Harlem where he meets friends who help him find his dog. Some simple Spanish phrases are introduced.

Liang, Yen. *Tommy and Dee-Dee.* New York: Henry Z. Walck, 1953. A simply written story illustrating how two boys living in different parts of the world are alike in many ways. Tommy is an American and Dee-Dee is Chinese.

Mao-chiu, Chang. *The little doctor.* Peking: Foreign Languages Press, 1965. Ping Ping, the little girl doctor helps make her sister's doll well, gives her brother's teddy bear a check up, and even repairs a broken rocking horse with hammer and nails. Typical story used with young children in China.*

Martin, Patricia Miles. *The rice bowl pet.* New York: Thomas Y. Crowell, 1962. Ah Jim lives in a crowded apartment in San Francisco Chinatown. He roams the streets looking for a pet small enough to fit in his rice bowl. Authentically illustrated by Ezra Jack Keats.

Moon, Grace, and Carl Moon. *One little Indian.* Chicago: Albert Whit-

---

* Chinese story books are written in English and are available from Guozi Shudian (China Publications Centre), P.O. Box 399, Peking, China. U.S. distributor: China Books & Periodicals, 125 Fifth Ave., New York, N.Y. 10003; 2929 Twenty-fourth St., San Francisco, Ca. 94110.

man, 1950. Ad-di wakes up feeling all shiny inside—it is his fifth birthday. Mother tells him that a surprise awaits him in the desert if he can find it. Children will enjoy the unexpected surprise that he finds.

Politi, Leo. *A boat for Peppe.* New York: Charles Scribner's Sons, 1950. Peppe's father, a Sicilian-American fisherman, is almost lost at sea. This story tells of Peppe's faith that his father will return and how he finally gets his wish for a boat. The setting of the book is Old Monterey, California.

_____. *Rosa.* New York: Charles Scribner's Sons, 1963. Rosa is a little girl who lives in San Felipe, Mexico. Her wish for a doll comes true in a special way when a baby sister is born on Christmas eve. The book is also available in Spanish.

_____. *Moy Moy.* New York: Charles Scribner's Sons, 1960. Authentic story of a little Chinese-American girl who celebrates Chinese New Year in Los Angeles. Includes some Chinese phrases.

Radlauer, Ed, and Ruth Radlauer. *Father is big.* Glendale, Ca: Bowmar, 1967. Close-up photographs by Harvey Mandlin show how a black child looks up to his father.

Scott, Ann Herbert. *On mother's lap.* New York: McGraw-Hill, 1972. The author of *Sam* has created another favorite. Michael, a young Eskimo boy, loves to rock on his mother's lap. But when the baby cries, he is sure there will not be enough room for both of them. Charming illustrations by Glo Coalson.

_____ (Symeon Shimin, illus.). *Sam.* New York: McGraw-Hill, 1967. Everyone in the family is too busy to pay any attention to Sam until he finally begins to cry. Then they find a job for him which is just right.

Showers, Paul. *Your skin and mine.* New York: Thomas Y. Crowell, 1965. This book shows three boys, Oriental, Negro, and Caucasian, examining and finding out about skin—how it protects you, different colors of skin, etc. This book is good for use with a small group of children in order to allow each one to share in the discussion. Illustrated by Paul Galdone.

Sonneborn, Ruth A. *Friday night is papa night.* New York: Viking, 1970. The tender story of a black family looking forward to having Papa come home on Friday night.

Steptoe, John. *Stevie.* New York: Harper & Row, 1969. Robert, a black child, is jealous when his mother takes care of a younger child, Stevie, in their home. The text is written as if Robert is telling the story. He learns about his sensitive feelings for Stevie when his mother no longer has to babysit.

Yashima, Taro. *Umbrella.* New York: Viking, 1958. Beautiful illustrations and text about a little Japanese girl, Momo, who lives in New York and how eager she is to use her new umbrella.

_____. *Youngest one.* New York: Viking, 1962. Two-year-old Bobby, the youngest member of the family, finally overcomes his shyness and ventures outside his familiar family group. He finds a friend in Momo. Children can identify with Bobby's feelings when he begins to make friends of his own. This is one of several beautifully illustrated stories about Japanese children in New York.

Yashima, Taro and Mitsu. *Momo's kitten.* New York: Viking, 1961. Momo finds a kitten who becomes her "nyan-nyan." She nurses her pet back to health and takes on new responsibilities when her cat becomes a mother.

Yi, Yang and Liang, Ko. *I am on duty today*. Peking: Foreign Languages Press, 1966. This simple story colorfully illustrated by Ku Yin shows a typical day in a Chinese nursery school where the little girl helps the teacher set up the classroom, do daily exercises, pass out pencils and paper, get the children ready for nap, and distribute the snacks. Very similar to activities in American schools, but this is a good example of how emphasis is placed on teaching cooperation and concern for others before oneself.*

Bibliographies of Multi-Ethnic Books

Griffin, Louise. *Multi-ethnic books for young children: annotated bibliography for parents and teachers.* Washington: National Association for the Education of Young Children for the ERIC Clearinghouse on Early Childhood Education, 1970. Books are annotated and categorized according to age groups. Ethnic books focus on American Indians and Eskimos, Appalachia and the Southern Mountains, Afro-Americans, Hawaii and the Philippines, Latin-American, Asian, Jewish and European. Included also are books for parents and teachers.

National Association for the Advancement of Colored People. *Integrated school books: a descriptive bibliography of 399 pre-school and elementary school texts and story books. New York: NAACP, 1967.*

White, Doris. *Multi-ethnic books for head start children, part I: black and integrated literature.* Also *Multi-ethnic books for head start children, part II: other minority group literature.* Urbana, Illinois: ERIC Clearinghouse on Early Childhood Education, 1969. Both booklets contain annotated lists of children's books and materials covering such subjects as poetry, fiction, folklore, music, math, science, social studies, health, adult readings, records, and films.

Christmas Stories

Ets, Marie Hall. *Nine days to Christmas*. New York: Viking, 1959. The story tells about Mexican customs at Christmastime. This is a Caldecott award winner. (See Multi-Ethnic Books for further description.)

Fraser, James (Nick De Grazia, illus.). *Las Posadas, a Christmas story.* Flagstaff, Ariz.: Northland Press, 1963. A simply written and illustrated story about the festival celebrated in Mexico nine days before Christmas.

Geisel, Theodor (Dr. Seuss, pseud.). *How the Grinch stole Christmas.* New York: Random House, 1957. Dr. Seuss' imaginative treatment of a grinch who tried to put a stop to Christmas. The rhythmic format is familiar to children and teachers who like to read Dr. Seuss books.

Moore, Clement C. (Leonard Weisgard, illus.). *The night before Christmas.* New York: Grosset & Dunlap, 1949. There are many treatments of this classic tale with this one being one of the most popular among teachers.

---

* See note on page 48.

Wenning, Elizabeth. *The Christmas mouse.* New York: Holt, Rinehart & Winston, 1959. This is a true story of "Silent Night, Holy Night" written in an appealing way for young children. Good for telling without a book and then showing the pictures afterward.

Easter Stories

Brown, Margaret Wise. *The golden egg book.* New York: Simon & Schuster, 1947. A beautiful, simply written story. Large, colorful illustrations.

Holl, Adelaide (Roger Duvoisin, illus.). *The remarkable egg.* New York: Lothrop, Lee & Shepard, 1968. A coot finds a round red egg in her nest and demands to know who laid it there.

Kraus, Robert. *Daddy long ears.* New York: Simon & Schuster, 1970. "Once there was a rabbit who was called Daddy Long Ears because he had many children and long ears. After the birth of their thirty-first child, Mrs. Long Ears ran away with a muskrat and Daddy Long Ears was left with thirty-one bunnies to be both father and mother to. It wasn't easy." An amusing and touching story of how a Daddy rabbit earned the title of Easter Rabbit.

Littlefield, William (Vladimir Bobri, illus.). *The whiskers of Ho Ho.* New York: Lothrop, Lee & Shepard, 1958. A Chinese tale about Kwang Fu, the old man and his hen who lays eggs and his rabbit who makes them beautiful for children everywhere.

Milhous, Katherine. *The egg tree.* New York: Charles Scribner's Sons, 1950. Children will want to help make their own egg tree after hearing this story. The teacher can use hollow decorated eggs to demonstrate. A Caldecott medal winner. A good book for the teacher to use in making an egg tree is *Easter eggs for everyone,* by Evelyn Coskey, New York: Abingdon, 1973.

Tresselt, Alvin (Roger Duvoisin, illus.). *The world in the candy egg.* New York: Lothrop, Lee & Shepard, 1967. The miniature landscape inside a candy egg is seen by a tiny bird, a chicken, a lamb, and a rabbit, but the make-believe world of the egg goes to a little girl.

Zolotow, Charlotte (Betty Peterson, illus.). *The bunny who found Easter.* Berkeley: Parnassus Press, 1959. A bunny goes searching through summer, autumn, and winter for Easter until he finds its true meaning in the spring. A good lap book.

Hallowe'en Stories

Adams, Adrienne. *A woggle of witches.* New York: Charles Scribner's Sons, 1971. On a certain night when the moon is high, all the witches fly on their brooms' way up into the dark sky. They have fun on their night out until they run into a parade of little monsters who frighten them. Beautifully imaginative illustrations.

Balian, Lorna. *Humbug witch.* New York: Abingdon, 1965. A little girl dresses up like a witch and tries to make magic potions with such things as paprika, hair tonic, pickle juice, peanut butter, etc. Can be adpated to the flannel board.

Bright, Robert. *Georgie's Halloween.* New York: Doubleday, 1958. One of a delightful series by Bright about Georgie, a friendly ghost.

1. *Invite parents to share stories and food to celebrate special holidays.*
2. *Contact local libraries, storytellers guild, book clubs to invite storytellers to school.*
3. *Encourage expression of feelings with words.*
4. *Send notes home to let parents know what books their children enjoy in school.*
5. *Suggest good books to buy for gifts.*
6. *Start a special fund to buy duplicate books for a lending library.*
7. *Make annotated lists of favorite stories available in the local library and suggest parents take their children.*
8. *Tell stories with slide transparencies.*

Calhoun, Mary. *Wobble, the witch cat.* New York: William Morrow, 1958. It wasn't easy for Wobble the witch cat to ride on his mistress's broom with the slippery handle. The thought of falling off again made him cranky enough to do some mean things, including pushing the broom into the trash barrel. Wobble has the last laugh when he flies by all the other witch cats riding comfortably on his vacuum cleaner.

Coombs, Patricia. *Dorrie's magic.* New York: Lothrop, Lee & Shepard, 1962. A little witch tries to find the right magic to clean her room.

Lasson, Robert. *Which witch?* New York: David McKay, 1959. "Once there were two witches. One was rich. The other had an itch." Children enjoy the silly antics of each witch, especially when the wrong magic words create streets full of ice cream.

Low, Alice. *Witch's holiday.* New York: Pantheon, 1971. A little boy's imaginary witches escape from his closet on Hallowe'en and create all kinds of mischief.

Varga, Judy. *Once-a-year witch.* New York: William Morrow, 1973. Booboolina the witch snatched every little girl she could find until the townspeople raided her cottage. What they discovered is the surprise. The clever plot suggests a way the custom of trick-or-treating may have started.

von Hippel, Ursula. *The craziest halloween.* New York: Coward-Mc-Cann, 1959. A little witch wants to prove that she is a real witch. Amusing.

Hanukkah Stories

Bial, Morrison David. *The Hanukkah story.* New York: Behrman House, 1952. This book gives instructions on how to play the dreidel game which children like.

Cedarbaum, Sophia N. *Chanuko.* New York: Union of Hebrew Congregations, 1960. Two children plan for the Chanuko festival. May not be appropriate for those who are unfamiliar with the holiday, but the teacher can use this for background material to adapt to her needs.

Morrow, Betty, and Louis Hartmon. *A holiday book of Jewish holidays.* Champaign, Ill.: Garrard, 1967. Easy explanations and readable history of Jewish holidays including Hanukkah, Purim, Passover, Yom Kippur, Rosh Hashanah. Good for teachers' background material.

Holiday Storybooks for the Teacher

The following books include some good selections of stories the teacher can learn for telling on special occasions.

The Child Study Association of America (compilers). *Holiday storybook.* New York: Thomas Y. Crowell, 1952. One of the few books containing stories about some of the less popular holidays. This book consists of stories on such holidays as Purim, Hanukkah, United Nations Day, Lincoln's Birthday, Labor Day, etc. Among some of the best for telling to preschoolers are "A Valentine Story," by Evelyn Davis; "Mr. Plum and the Little Green Tree," by Helen Earle Gilbert (Arbor Day); and "Horace the Happy Ghost," by Elizabeth Ireland (Hallowe'en). Very few illustrations.

Purcell, John Wallace. *The true book of holidays and special days.* Chicago: Children's Press, 1955. This book gives a brief description of each holiday and why we celebrate it.

Books About Shapes

Atwood, Ann. *The little circle.* New York: Charles Scribner's Sons, 1967. A story about a little circle who starts out being a zero and goes through a series of adventures, becoming the circle of a daisy, a nest in a tree, a ripple in a fountain of water, and many other circles found in nature. Lovely color photographs.

Budney, Blossom. *A kiss is round.* New York: Lothrop, Lee & Shepard, 1954. Colorful illustrations of common objects which are round—a ring, balloon, pie, doughnut, money, clock, etc.

Charosh, Mannis. *The ellipse.* New York: Thomas Y. Crowell, 1971. An ellipse is a flattened circle. If you point a flashlight beam directly at a darkened wall you will see a circle, but if you tip the flashlight up just a little you will see an ellipse. This book has many similar simple experiments that young children can do. This is one in the series of Young Math Books edited by Dr. Max Beberman to acquaint the child with such concepts as *Bigger and Smaller, Odds and Evens,* and *Circles.*

Feltser, Eleanor B. *The Sesame Street book of shapes.* New York: Preschool Press, Time-Life Books, 1970. Photographs and illustrations developed from material provided by the Sesame Street series so well known on television.

Hoban, Tana. *Shapes and things.* New York: Macmillan, 1970. Common articles such as comb, brush, hammer, letters in white on black background without words.

Lerner, Sharon. *Square is a shape.* Minneapolis: Lerner, 1970. Different shapes done in torn colored paper.

Matthiesen, Thomas. *Things to see: a child's world of familiar objects.* New York: Platt & Monk, 1966. Lovely color photography of familiar objects.

Shapur, Fredun. *Round and round and square.* London: Abelard-Schuman, 1965. Circles and squares illustrated in primary colors showing how different shapes can be made from parts of the basic shapes. A square can be cut into triangles and parts of triangles and circles can make houses, kites, etc.

Books About Numbers

McLeod, Emile. *One snail and me.* Boston: Little, Brown, 1961. A good book to use with one child or small group so children can look for the snail on each page.

Oxenbury, Helen. *Numbers of things.* New York: Franklin Watts, 1968. The child can count the number of colorful illustrations on each page, such as two cars, four mice. Good for one child with adult. The illustrations encourage putting finger on each object while the child counts.

Slobodkin, Louis. *Millions and millions and millions!* New York: Vanguard Press, 1955. Large, colorfully illustrated book calling attention to the fact that there are millions of stars and millions of cars, millions of other common things, but there is only one you and one me.

Steiner, Charlotte. *Ten in a family.* New York: Alfred A. Knopf, 1960. This teaches adding and subtracting as well as counting from one to ten. Can be adapted for use with a flannel board.

Ungerer, Tomi. *One, two, where's my shoe?* New York: Harper & Row, 1964. The artist disguises drawings of all kinds of shoes in his illustrations and the child must go on a pictorial search through the pages. Good for use with one or two children.

————. *Snail, where are you?* New York: Harper & Row, 1962. Same format as above except the snail is hidden in illustrations.

Wildsmith, Brian. *Brian Wildsmith's 1,2,3's.* New York: Franklin Watts, 1965. Numbers are illustrated with bright shapes, such as one colorful circle, five different size triangles, etc. The combinations of numbers, shapes, and forms may be confusing for the beginner.

Books About Colors

Freeman, Don. *A rainbow of my own.* New York: Viking, 1966. A child sees a rainbow and runs out to catch it for his own. This is a book to encourage the imagination and interest in colors.

Hoffmann, Beth Greiner. *Red is for apples.* New York: Random House, 1966. A book in rhyme calling attention to familiar objects and their colors.

Lionni, Leo. *Little blue and little yellow.* New York: Astor-Honor, 1959. Torn paper illustrations showing how two colors can make a third. Good for adapting for use on the flannel board with cellophane or tissue paper mounted on flannel or sandpaper frames.

Wolff, Robert J. *Hello yellow!* New York: Charles Scribner's Sons, 1968. This is the third book of Robert Wolff's about primary colors. *Seeing red* and *feeling blue* also translate colors into familiar objects and abstract images.

Books About the ABC's

Alexander, Anne. *ABC of cars and trucks.* New York: Doubleday, 1956. A favorite, especially with little boys who enjoy looking at the cars and trucks.

Bond, Susan. *Ride with me, through ABC.* New York: Scroll Press, 1968.

Gag, Wanda. *The ABC bunny.* New York: Coward McCann, 1933. This is an old-time favorite with original lithographs and hand lettering.

Munari, Bruno. *ABC.* New York: World, 1960. Clear, bright, simple, and large illustrations.

Turlay, Clare Newberry. *The kittens' ABC.* New York: Harper & Row, 1965. Reissue of a favorite large book with illustrations of kittens on each page.

Wildsmith, Brian. *Brian Wildsmith's ABC.* New York: Franklin Watts, 1962. Large, modern, colorful illustrations each accompanied by a word in upper case and lower case letters.

Books About Community Workers

Rubinger, Michael. *I know an astronaut.* New York: G. P. Putnam's Sons, 1972. A little boy accompanies his Uncle Bill, an astronaut, to the space center, where he takes a tour and learns about the kind of work astronauts do. This book is one of the Community Helper Books published by G. P. Putnam's Sons to acquaint the young child with various community workers. Written and illustrated by different authors, titles include *I know a policeman, I know a librarian, I know a bank teller, I know a teacher.* A good series of "Let's Visit" books illustrated with photos of children visiting such places and people as the hospital, doctor's office, supermarket, police and fire station, etc., is published by Taylor Publishing Company (Your World Series), Dallas, Texas.

Books for Children About Death

Brown, Margaret Wise. *The dead bird.* New York: Young Scott Books, 1938 and 1965. A simple story touchingly illustrated by Remy Charlip about some children who find a dead bird and bury it in the woods. The description of death is factual and handles the subject in a way that a child can understand and accept.

de Paola, Tomie. *Nana upstairs & Nana downstairs.* New York: G. P. Putnam's Sons, 1973. "Nana Downstairs kept busy in the kitchen by the big black stove. Nana Upstairs rested in her bedroom. She was ninety-four years old. Tommy loved visiting them on Sunday afternoons. But one day, when Tommy ran up the steps to see Nana Upstairs, her bedroom was empty. This is the heart warming and very real story of that special relationship between the very young and the very old and the moment when the two must part."

Fassler, Joan. *My grandpa died today.* New York: Behavioral Publications, 1971. Realistic treatment of a young boy's close relationship with his grandfather and his adjustment to the grandfather's death.

Written by a child psychologist. Look for other books from this publisher's series dealing with "sensitive" topics.

Freschet, Burneice. *The old bullfrog.* New York: Charles Scribner's Sons, 1968. A beautifully written book about the understanding of survival.

Harris, Audrey. *Why did he die?* Minneapolis: Lerner, 1965. A mother's poem explaining to her child about the death of his friend's grandfather. Good for use with young children. Unusual because the story deals with the death of a human being.

Kantrowitz, Mildred. *When Violet died.* New York: Parents' Magazine Press, 1973. They knew Violet was going to die, so when the little bird lay down in her cage, the children gave her a burial and wake with songs, poems, and strawberry punch.

Miles, Miska. *Annie and the old one.* Boston: Little, Brown, 1971. When the new rug is taken from the loom, Annie's grandmother, The Old One, will return to Mother Earth. Her family all understood the cycle of nature, but Annie couldn't. A poignant story of a little Navajo girl and her very special relationship with her grandmother. Lovely illustrations by Peter Parnall of life in a hogan. Read with small group or one child.

Viorst, Judith. *The tenth good thing about Barney.* New York: Atheneum, 1971. A young boy tenderly narrates the story of his pet's death. He must remember ten good things about his cat, Barney, to tell at the funeral. Realistic treatment of the death of a pet and how the boy comes to deal with his loss.

Books for Children About Divorce

Adams, Florence. *Mushy eggs.* (See description under "Books About Other Childhood Experiences.") Children of divorced parents are saddened by the departure of their very special baby sitter.

Goff, Beth. *Where is daddy?* Boston: Beacon Press, 1969. Very few stories are written for the preschooler about divorce. This one was written by a psychiatric social worker to help a child adjust to her parents' divorce. This story is good for reading aloud on a one-to-one basis, giving the child plenty of opportunity to discuss and identify with the child in the story. An honest, realistic treatment of a difficult subject for the young child to understand.

Lexau, Joan M. *Me day.* New York: Dial Press, 1971. Rafer wakes up on his birthday with good feelings inside, but he quickly grows disappointed. His parents are divorced and he has not heard from his father. Then his mother sends him on a mysterious errand. . . . Children can identify with Rafer's reaction to his parents' divorce and how important the celebration of a special day can be. Written in black dialect style, the text may be too wordy at times for a preschooler. Good for discussion of feelings.

Sex Education Books for Children

Andry, Andrew C. *How babies are made.* New York: Time-Life Books, 1968. Honest answers to children's questions about sex. Photographs of colored cut-out paper.

De Schweinitz, Karl. *Growing up.* New York: Macmillan, 1965. One of the best books for preschoolers dealing with the topic of growing up. Good for use with one child or a small group in order to allow for discussion.

Gruenberg, Sidonie Matsner. *The wonderful story of how you were born.* New York: Doubleday, 1970. Good book to look at with a child but too many words for the preschooler. Use this for the excellent illustrations showing sperm, ovum, fetus.

Manushkin, Fran. *Baby.* New York: Harper & Row, 1972. Mrs. Tracy was growing a baby and baby didn't want to be born. Humorously illustrated tale showing the various positions and facial expressions of a baby inside the mommy and its responses to other members of the family waiting for it to be born. Pictures by Ronald Himler.

Selsam, Millicent E. *How puppies grow.* New York: Four Winds Press, 1971. Actual photographs by Esther Bubley showing six newborn pups and how they grow until they are old enough to be adopted.

Sheffield, Margaret. *Where do babies come from?* New York: Alfred A. Knopf, 1973. This is a very explicit book designed for use by parents with their children. Simple, direct explanations of conception, reproduction, and the life cycle. Sheila Bewley's softly colorful illustrations convey feelings of tenderness and warmth. Adapted from the award-winning B.B.C. program of the same title in England, this is by far the most honest book available on sex education for children.

Showers, Paul and Kay Sperry Showers. *Before you were a baby.* New York: Thomas Y. Crowell, 1968. Simply written and well illustrated book appropriate for use with preschoolers. Allow plenty of time for discussion.

Stories About a New Baby in the House

Arnstein, Helene S. *Billy and our new baby.* New York: Behavioral Publications, 1973. A good book for preschoolers who must deal with feelings of jealousy over the new baby. Billy acts out his conflicts by being aggressive, by crying, by regressing to bottle feeding. He learns that it's all right to have angry feelings, but that he may not hurt others. Gradually, Billy's parents help him to understand his importance in the family. There is a helpful guide at the end with suggestions and information about sibling rivalry.

Borack, Barbara. *Someone small.* New York: Harper & Row, 1969. A child's daily experiences with a new baby in the house and with her bird that dies.

Hoban, Russell. *A baby sister for Frances.* New York: Harper & Row, 1964. This is one of several books about a badger named Frances. When a new baby comes to the house Frances is unhappy because she does not get enough attention.

Holland, Vicki. *We are having a baby.* New York: Charles Scribner's Sons, 1971. Four-year-old Dana is just as excited as her mother and father about the birth of their baby. But when the baby arrives at home, Dana is not sure if she likes the idea. Dana narrates the story, and the expressive photographs capture her reactions to this new event.

Iwasaki, Chihiro. *A new baby is coming to my house.* New York: McGraw-Hill, 1970. A young girl muses about the arrival of a new baby brother. What will he look like? What can she give him for a present? Lovely watercolor illustrations complement simple text.

Keats, Ezra Jack. *Peter's chair.* New York: Harper & Row, 1967. Peter's old cradle, high chair, and crib are all painted pink for his new baby sister. He is so unhappy that he decides to take his little blue chair and run away from home.

Langstaff, Nancy. *A tiny baby for you.* New York: Harcourt, Brace & World, 1955. A boy learns to accept a new baby in the house. Good photography by Suzanne Szasz.

Schick, Eleanor. *Peggy's new brother.* New York: Macmillan, 1970. Peggy tries to be helpful with her new baby brother, but everything she does goes wrong.

Schlein, Miriam. *Laurie's new brother.* London: Abelard-Schuman, 1961. Laurie is accustomed to having mommy and daddy all to herself, so she resents her new baby brother because he takes so much of their time. She gradually becomes adjusted to his presence.

Stories About Moving to a New Home

Felt, Sue. *Hello-goodbye.* New York: Doubleday, 1960. Candace and her baby sister have to move because their daddy has been transferred. Candace is unhappy about leaving. Illustrations show the routine of moving and how the girls make new friends after they move.

Hoff, Syd. *Who will be my friend?* New York: Harper & Row, 1960. Freddy's problem was how to find friends in a new town. He plays ball by himself until the boys notice how good he is. This is simply written for the early reader.

Marino, Dorothy. *That's my favorite.* Philadelphia: J. B. Lippincott, 1956. Suzy moves into a city apartment and looks for a friend. She plays hopscotch, jumprope, skates, and plays with four girls who are quadruplets.

Viklund, Alice R. *Moving away.* New York: McGraw Hill, 1967. One of the best books available on the subject of moving. This is a small book, easy to hold, sensitively written and delicately illustrated. "Moving away is leaving behind people and places you know so well. It is a time when everything is different." "It is a time to put things in boxes, decide which toys to take with you, and who to give your goldfish to. . . ." The child discovers that a new home can be nice too and that things are not so different.

Wise, William. *The house with the red roof.* New York: G. P. Putnam's Sons, 1961. Jimmy likes his house with the red roof and all the familiar things about his life. He thinks he is going to live there forever, but one day his father tells him they are moving far away. He is reluctant, uncertain, but after the routine of moving he discovers he doesn't mind his new house with the brown roof.

Books About Other Childhood Experiences

Adams, Florence. *Mushy eggs.* New York: G. P. Putnam's Sons, 1973. "Since they visit Dad only on the weekends and Mom works everyday in the city, Fanny is a very special person to Sam and David. And one afternoon, when she tells them she is returning to Italy, they realize just how awful it feels to have someone you love go away."

Babbitt, Natalie. *The something.* New York: Farrar, Straus, & Giroux, 1970. Mylo the monster is afraid of the dark—or rather, of The Something he believes will come in through his window at night. His mother gives him some clay to make a statue of The Something. Mylo begins to wish The Something would appear so that he could make a better likeness. One night he has a dream and meets The Something. Mylo finds he is no longer afraid and decides to keep the statue next to his bed. Children may be amused at the prospect of a monster being afraid. Creative resolution to a child's fears.

Berger, Knute; Robert A. Tidwell, and Margaret Haseltine. *A visit to the doctor.* New York: Grossett & Dunlap, 1960. A detailed discussion about a child going to the doctor for a physical examination, with illustrations of the little boy getting his height, weight, temperature, and pulse recorded; the doctor listens to his chest with a stethoscope and he gets a booster injection. The text is factual and written for the young child but there may be too many explanations for the three-year-old. Good to use as a basis for discussion.

Bradbury, Ray. *Switch on the night.* New York: Pantheon Books, 1955. A little boy overcomes his fears of the dark by learning to "switch on" the night—seeing and hearing the crickets, frogs, stars, and moon come alive.

Chase, Francine. *A visit to the hospital.* New York: Grosset & Dunlap, 1957. This is a well written and accurately illustrated book about a boy who goes to the hospital to have his tonsils removed. A shorter version of this same book is published under the same title by Wonder Books, 1958.

Cohen, Miriam. *Will I have a friend?* New York: Macmillan, 1967. Jim wonders if he will have a friend at nursery school. The children easel paint, play with clay, have juice and stories and when Jim goes home he realizes he has a friend at school.

Collier, James Lincoln. *Danny goes to the hospital.* New York: W. W. Norton, 1970. Actual photographs of a little boy who goes to the hospital to have an operation to repair a damaged eye muscle. Pictures show different people and parts of the hospital as well as the things that happen to Danny.

Garn, Bernard J. *A visit to the dentist.* New York: Grosset & Dunlap, 1959. Illustrations and text of a little boy who goes to the dentist for a regular checkup. Many details and factual information. If this book is too wordy, the same publisher has a shorter version in its Wonder Book series (1959) under the same title and author.

Gauch, Patricia Lee. *Grandpa and me.* New York: Coward, McCann & Geoghegan, 1972. Story describes the special relationship between a grandparent and a child. Beautiful pencil/wash drawings by Shimin.

Hurd, Edith Thacher. *Come with me to nursery school.* New York: Coward, McCann, 1970. "What will I do at my school?" A collection of photographs by Edward Bigelow along with the text show everyday activities in nursery school setting. Useful to help introduce children to nursery school.

Hutchins, Pat. *Titch.* New York: Macmillan, 1971. Titch's older brother and sister always have bigger and better things than he does. They have bicycles and he has only a tricycle; they have kites while he has a pinwheel. But when the threesome decide to plant a tree, Titch becomes the "hero" because he has the seed. Bright, simple illustrations accompany the sparse text.

Iwasaki, Chihiro. *Staying home alone on a rainy day.* New York:

McGraw-Hill, 1968. Beautiful illustrations of a girl who finds things to do around the house until her mother comes home.

Memling, Carl. *What's in the dark?* New York: Parents' Magazine Press, 1971. "What's in the dark? After they've clicked the light off. . . ." Shadows on the wall, moon in the sky, animals asleep, trucks on the street. The dark of night becomes more familiar and less frightening to the child. Big, bright illustrations accompany simple text.

Merriam, Eve. *Mommies at work.* New York: Alfred A. Knopf, 1955. Summarizes the various careers and jobs mothers have, from domestic skills to working in an assembly line, being a doctor, and many more.

Paullin, Ellen. *No more tonsils!* Boston: Beacon Press, 1958. Good photography of a little girl going to the hospital to have her tonsils taken out.

Rockwell, Harlow. *My doctor.* New York: Macmillan, 1973. Story of a child's first visit to a doctor's office. The doctor reassuringly tells the child how she will use each of her instruments for the check-up.

Serfozo, Mary. *Welcome Roberto.* Chicago: Follett, 1969. A Mexican-American child's first experience in school.

Shay, Arthur. *What happens when you go to the hospital.* Chicago: Reilly & Lee, 1969. Photographs of a black girl named Karen who goes to the hospital for two days to have her tonsils removed. Details show routine procedures of taking temperature, blood test, x-rays, etc., and finally the operating room and recovery.

Showers, Paul. *How many teeth?* New York: Thomas Y. Crowell, 1962. Well written book on learning about the teeth and their care.

Silverstein, Shel. *The giving tree.* New York: Harper & Row, 1964. A touching parable which tells of the child who took more and more from his tree—the apples, its branches, its wood, until there was only a stump left. A sad and effective interpretation of "the gift of giving and a serene acceptance of another's capacity to love in return."

Simon, Norma. *I know what I like.* Chicago: Whitman, 1971. This well-written book helps the young child to be more sensitive to the feelings and ideas of others—ideas that may be quite different from his own. It also encourages an acceptance of one's own feelings. A good book to use for discussion and further exploration and expression of feelings.

Skorpen, Liesel Moak. *All the Lassies.* New York: Dial Press, 1970. Peter wants a dog for a pet, but his parents try to persuade him to have another animal. He ends up with a fish, a turtle, a bird, and a cat, all of which he names Lassie. Finally, Peter gets his wish for a dog, and he chooses the largest dog in the pet shop and names it Walter! Charming pencil sketches by Bruce Martin Scott.

Sonneborn, Ruth A. *The lollipop party.* New York: Viking, 1967. Tomas has to stay home alone and wait for his mother to return from work. He is scared and holds his cat for comfort. But Tomas's fears are relieved when his nursery school teacher comes to visit. They have a lollipop party in honor of the occasion.

Tamburine, Jean. *I think I will go to the hospital.* New York: Abingdon, 1965. Susy doesn't want to go to the hospital to have her tonsils out. She plays hospital with her pets and visits friends who have been hospitalized and soon realizes that the hospital is a good place to be when you are sick.

Watson, Jane Werner; Switzer, Robert E.; J. Cotter Hirschberg. New

York: Western, 1971. These authors have written a series of books in cooperation with the Menninger Foundation for Solving Problems of Childhood (Read-Together Book for Parents and Children). Some of the titles include *Sometimes I get angry, Sometimes I'm afraid, Sometimes I get jealous*. A worthwhile series to use in discussing feelings.

Zolotow, Charlotte. *A father like that*. New York: Harper & Row, 1971. "I wish I had a father. But my father went away. . . ." A boy imagines what his father would be like. A touching story of a child's imaginary ideal family.

————. *William's doll*. New York: Harper & Row, 1972. William wanted a doll more than anything else. His family tried to discourage him. Only William's grandmother understood how he felt. Sympathetic treatment, although text may be a bit wordy for preschoolers. Color illustrations by William Pene Du Bois.

Picture Books Without Words

The following are excellent "lap" books which encourage language development and use of the imagination. They are used most effectively with one child at a time.

Alexander, Martha. *Bobo's dream*. New York: Dial Press, 1970. Bobo is a dachshund whose master saves his bone from a large mongrel. Bobo dreams of returning the favor. Martha Alexander's first book without words *Out! out! out!* is another excellent selection.

Amoss, Berthe. *By the sea*. New York: Parents' Magazine Press, 1969. A fantasy of line drawings showing children at the beach. The hero wears red trunks, holds a red kite, and has a dog with a red collar. The kite pulls the little boy up into the sky and the little dog goes after him with a red balloon. This is a small book, fun for little hands to hold.

Goodall, John S. *The adventures of Paddy Pork*. New York: Harcourt, Brace & World, 1968. A charmingly illustrated book in detailed black and white line drawings of a pig who runs away to join the circus. A second book by the same author, also without words, is *The ballooning adventures of Paddy Pork* (1969) which has our hero saving a piglet from a band of gorillas. Good for use with children who have had exposure to many stories and will not be frightened by ferocious looking animals.

————. *The midnight adventures of Kelly, Dot, and Esmeralda*. New York: Atheneum, 1972. Soft, detailed watercolors without words tells the story of three toys, a Koala bear, a doll, and a mouse, who wake up at midnight and begin their adventures by climbing into a landscape picture on the wall. The effective use of half-pages heightens the child's interest and imagination. A good lap book to share with one child.

Hoban, Tana. *Look again!* New York: Macmillan, 1971. Look once, look twice. Look again! Collection of black and white photographs in an amusing format. Illustrates there is more than one way of seeing a picture. Children enjoy guessing the surprise answers. Good for language involvement. Look for other books by Hoban on teaching concepts (*Push, pull, empty, full; Count and see; Shapes and things*).

Mayer, Mercer. *A boy, a dog and a frog*. New York: Dial Press, 1967. A small book with delightful drawings of a boy and his dog and their

> *1. Choose a story you like.*
> *2. Choose a story that is easy to memorize (for example,* Caps for Sale*).*
> *3. No need to memorize word for word, but stick to the plot.*
> *4. Repeat the story to yourself while driving, doing the dishes, etc.*
> *5. Visualize the incidents in your story.*
> *6. Watch the children and speak directly to them.*
> *7. Use pauses for effect.*
> *8. Show enthusiasm.*
> *9. Don't add your own comments.*

attempt to catch a frog for a pet. The sequel to this book is *Frog, where are you?* (1969) which shows the frog escaping from a jar at night and the little boy and his dog finding their friend in the pond.

————. *Bubble, bubble.* New York: Parents' Magazine Press, 1973. A little boy buys a magic bubble-maker and blows bubbles in all kinds of shapes, including some scary animals. But he can always pop his bubbles—or can he?

Simmons, Ellie. *Dog.* New York: David McKay, 1967. This is one of several books by the same author in the category of books "you can read before you know how." This is a simple story of a loving friendship between a boy and his new dog and the loneliness the boy feels when they have to be separated for a short time. Other titles by the same author are *Mary changes her clothes; Mary, the mouse champion; Cat; Wheels;* and *Family.* This last book (1970) shows the life of little girls whose mother is about to have a baby. Grandmother comes to stay and she and the little girls bake cakes, play cards, etc. until mother comes home with the new baby. All of these are small-sized books.

Wezel, Peter. *The good bird.* New York: Harper & Row, 1964. This is a large colorfully illustrated book about a bird who makes friends with a fish in a gold fish bowl by sharing a worm. See also *The naughty bird,* New York: Follett, 1967.

Language Activity Books for the Teacher*

Engel, Rose C. *Language motivating experiences for young children.* Van Nuys, Ca.: DFA Publishers, 1968. This book of activities provides "recipes" for the different areas in a preschool program, such as art, dramatic play, science, etc. Each of these activities is accompanied by suggestions for things to talk about. The introduction includes a discussion of the acquisition of language and speech and the role of the teacher. The appendix provides some evaluation materials and books for the teacher.

Karnes, Merle B. *Helping young children develop language skills.* Arlington, Virginia: The Council for Exceptional Children, 1968. This is a very good book covering such areas of language as listening skills,

---

* Chapter 9 of text provides additional information and a bibliography about language development.

motor expression, auditory and visual memory, etc. Each chapter includes suggestions for activities and games to use with the child.

Schubert, Delwyn G. (ed.). *Reading games that teach.* Monterey Park, Ca.: Creative Teaching Press, 1965. A series of teaching games designed to reinforce reading skills. Some of these are for older children who can read, but many can be adapted for use in the preschool. Games in the readiness section include suggestions for activities which require the child to tell "what happened next," select the "best path for bunny," and "cover the odd one."

Storytelling Books for the Teacher

The teacher who has told a story without the use of props will appreciate the unique experience she and her children share together. No longer does she have to contend with "Teacher, I can't see the picture!" or children on the fringes of a group disrupting the rest of the children while the teacher reads to them with her face turned away from the action. The teacher is free to maintain eye contact with the children and the children are free from all distractions of a book or pictures so that they may concentrate on the spoken words. The following books provide guidelines and suggestions for helping the teacher tell a story. The bibliography of story books for children also indicates those stories which lend themselves easily to storytelling.

Carlson, Bernice Wells. *Listen! and help tell the story.* New York: Abingdon, 1965. The emphasis of this book is on encouraging the child to listen and participate in telling a story. The contents include sections on finger plays, action verses, action stories, poems and stories with sound effects, poems with a refrain and with a chorus. Some can be easily memorized by the teacher; others can be used with the book.

Cohen, Monroe D. (ed.). *Literature with children.* Washington, D.C.: Association for Childhood Education International, 1972. This booklet contains short, helpful articles by outstanding authors covering such subjects as the classics, poetry, storytelling, dramatizing literature, creative experiences, using multimedia with literature, and teacher resources.

Cundiff, Ruby Ethel, and Barbara Webb. *Story-telling for you: a handbook of help for storytellers everywhere.* Yellow Springs, Ohio: Antioch, 1957. A very helpful book with step-by-step procedure on selection of an appropriate story for the audience, preparation, rehearsal, and presentation of the story. There is a section of questions and answers and a selected bibliography with some samples.

Sawyer, Ruth. *The way of the storyteller.* New York: Viking, 1962. This is not a book on "how to tell stories and what to tell" according to the author, but every teacher should be familiar with Ruth Sawyer's philosophy on the creative art of storytelling.

Fingerplay and Flannel Board Books for the Teacher

Anderson, Paul S., *Storytelling with the flannel board.* Minneapolis: T. S. Denison, 1963. Flannel boards are an almost foolproof method of presenting stories and learning materials to young children. The new teacher also finds that flannel board materials provide her with the security she needs to maintain the interest of a group of children. The flannel pictures are usually easier for all to see than a picture

> *1. Glue bits of Velcro to tips of garden gloves (Velcro can be purchased in fabric stores or notions).*
> *2. Cut figures to represent fingerplay characters (soldiers, bees, pumpkins) out of flannel or construction paper.*
> *3. Back the figures with Velcro.*
> *4. Attach and detach these to your gloves as you do finger plays.*

book; the visual attention of the audience is focused on the board rather than the teacher who may be self conscious, and the pictures serve as an outline and reminder for the teacher so she need not memorize as much as necessary for storytelling without aids. The author is helpful in making suggestions and providing guidelines for the selection and preparation of stories which lend themselves to use with the flannel board. There are instructions and patterns for making a flannel board as well as stories and patterns for characters to accompany each story.

Ellis, Mary Jackson. *Fingerplay approach to dramatization.* Minneapolis; T. S. Denison, 1960. Fingerplays encourage listening and participating in "small stories." They help in the development of small muscle coordination, promote speech and development of vocabulary. Children love them and every teacher should have a good repertoire of finger plays for all occasions. This book provides helpful suggestions to the teacher and includes well-illustrated finger plays on such topics as Halloween, raindrops, little seeds, snowflakes, etc. Dramatizations also include total body involvement.

————, and Frances Lyons. *Finger playtime.* Minneapolis: T. S. Denison, 1960. Simple rhyming finger plays with illustrations. Jingles cover topics such as "Two Little Kittens," "My Toothbrush," "The Fire Engine," and "Our Little Baby."

Scott, Louise Binder, and J. J. Thompson. *Rhymes for fingers and flannelboards.* St. Louis: Webster Division, McGraw-Hill, 1960. This book includes an interesting introduction regarding finger plays of long ago, value of finger plays, suggestions and purpose and devices the teacher can use. Descriptions of suggested materials to use in acting out a rhyme and illustrations of figures to prepare for the flannelboard are included as well as a section on fingerplays in foreign languages; other sections focus on holidays, numbers, active and quiet times, and others.

Steiner, Violette G. and Roberta Evatt Pond. *Finger play fun.* Columbus, Ohio: Charles E. Merrill, 1970. A collection of old and new finger plays with photographs or illustrations accompanying each one. Sections include those on quiet time, counting, animals, holidays.

Wagner, Joseph Anthony. *Flannelboard teaching aids.* Belmont, Ca.: Fearon, 1960. A helpful booklet to provide the teacher with suggestions and aids for using the flannelboard in the classroom.

Where to Write for Additional Resource Materials

The following organizations will provide bibliographies of books, records, tapes, and other helpful resource aids. Some of the pamphlets are free and others cost a small fee. Inquire about specifics.

American Library Association, Children's Service Division
50 East Huron Street
Chicago, Illinois 60611

Association for Childhood Education International
3615 Wisconsin Avenue, N.W.
Washington, D.C. 20016

Association of Children's Librarians of Northern California
San Francisco Public Library
San Francisco, California 94102

The Child Study Association of America, Inc.
9 East 89th Street
New York, New York 10028

Encyclopedia Brittanica Educational Corporation
Reference Division
425 North Michigan Avenue
Chicago, Illinois 60611

National Association for the Education of Young Children
1834 Connecticut Avenue, N.W.
Washington, D.C. 20009

Two excellent aids for the teacher published by NAEYC in conjunction with ERIC are *Books in pre-school,* a guide to selecting, purchasing, and using children's books, and *Multi-ethnic books for young children,* an annotated bibliography for parents and teachers. Both were compiled by Louise Griffin.

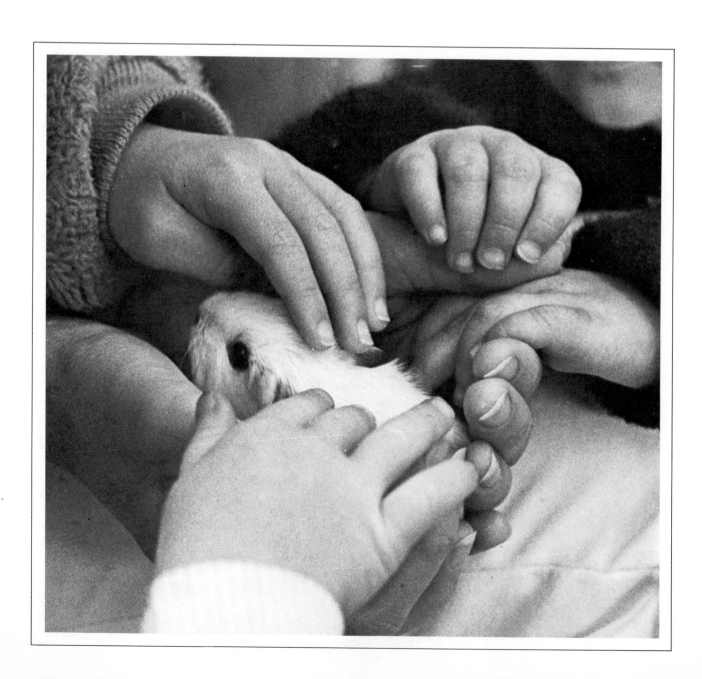

Part 2/ Experiences in Science

Introduction

Young children constantly explore the world around them. This exploration helps them gain concepts about the physical world. Satisfying their curiosity is essential for cognitive development and for their comprehension of order and relationships within their environment. The purpose of providing experiences in science is to assist the child in being more thorough and systematic in (1) gaining knowledge about the physical world, (2) becoming aware of the properties of objects and basic "laws" (such as gravity), and (3) developing skills to investigate and understand simple but basic ideas on which science is based.

Science grows out of *observations,* the forming of *hypotheses* and *experiments* to test these hypotheses, and *measurement* of results. All of these scientific operations have or can have their simple antecedents in the child's exploration of his environment. The child observes and records (though not systematically) his ideas about why things happen (the trees move and make the wind blow), tries out things to see if they work, and sees what happens as a result of what he has done. The teacher can help him do these things deliberately so that he may learn more from these experiences.

For example, she can direct and assist him to inquire and help develop skills to investigate and note independently such things as:

Causal relationships—one thing happens *because* something else happened first—that is, it is the result; it has been caused. When the teacher gives him a push on the swing, a certain back and forth movement follows. If he "pumps," the motion is maintained. If he stops, the motion stops.

Predictability of results—if the child drops a block from his hand, it will fall to the floor. If he does it ten times, he can be certain that the block will fall to the floor every time. Other things are not so predictable—if he drops a ball it will bounce back up fairly straight; if he drops a football, it may bounce straight up or bounce to the side; if he rolls dice or flips a coin, it is not always possible to predict which side will turn up.

The child should be given experiences and experiments he may not completely understand but which will give him the basis for future knowledge. The principle of conservation—that matter may change in form and composition but continues to exist—is not an easy concept to teach, but there are many examples of such transformations which the teacher can use to give him the knowledge and experimental base. The changing of water into ice is one example; the water is still there but in different form. Another is the difference in reactions that take place when sugar is put into one glass of water and sand into another glass of water. The sugar seems to disappear but is still in the water, as the child can observe by tasting it, etc. It is important that children have experiences that begin to lead them to new levels of understanding, even though these levels may not be reached until after they leave nursery school.

The teacher can distinguish between experiments which deal with objects and properties of the environment and the laws and principles which govern the operation of the physical world. It is one thing to help children learn about eggs, seeds, etc., and another to help them grasp the concept of reproduction—that all living things have ways to make new members of their own kind. This distinction between *objects* and *principles* is significant in that children can much more easily learn about the properties of objects than about the principles which govern the world around them.

Most of the tasks suggested here are designed to draw on resources that exist in the natural environment of the school or home. They allow for maximum participation by the child and they encourage independent investigation. The teacher needs to remember that the child is an active investigator, not a passive observer. By asking pertinent questions herself, she can teach him to phrase questions which will help him to make discoveries on his own. Different kinds of questions call for quite different types of responses. Questions which begin with words such as "Can . . ." or "Is . . ." or "Will . . ." or "Did . . ." can often be answered by a "yes" or "no." Questions which include words such as "Why . . ." "How . . ." call for much more complex answers and are usually very difficult for young children to answer. Questions such as "Who . . ." "What . . ." "When . . ." may often have specific answers of information and may or may not be easy to answer. The teacher's task, obviously, is to use those questions to which the child can respond. She may ask, "Does the ball always fall to the floor?" and expect a reasonable reply from a young child. If she asks, "Why does the ball fall to the floor?" she will only mystify and confuse. If she asks, "When (how soon) does the ball fall?" the child will probably be able to respond in a way that makes sense to both him and the teacher. She may ask, "What does a tadpole turn into?" and expect the child to know or to learn the answer; if she asks, "How does a tadpole become a frog?" she'll not get very far. The point in selecting questions carefully is to phrase them so that they are answerable for the child or will lead him to find the answer.

Having a science table or discovery corner provides opportunities for the child to explore. This can be used to display rocks, plants, a terrarium or aquarium, and many other interesting things to feel, smell, listen to, look at, and experiment with. The table can be changed to offer varied learning experiences. Children can be encouraged to bring their own contributions to share. Occasionally selecting a theme for science, such as "changes," "how things feel," or "growing things" may be useful. The activities in class could center around that particular theme. For "changes" the teacher might wish to make cinnamon toast for snack time and talk about how the bread changes to toast, in what ways boys and girls can and can't change as they grow, how leaves change color in different seasons. The science table can reflect the same theme with displays of how a dry sponge changes in water, how a starfish can grow back an arm, etc. Pictures on this same theme can be displayed.

Teaching science need not be formal. Every teacher has the opportunity to do some spontaneous teaching during the daily school routine. A snail from the garden, a bird's nest some child may have found, some sea shells from a recent trip—each provides the teacher and child an opportunity to gain more scientific information. When a school has many kinds of animals, the children will learn why they need food and water like humans do, how animals are born and grow, why and how the pigeon died, and what death means.

The outside environment presents many areas for discovery—why the leaves change colors and die and drift to the ground, how a bud blossoms into a flower, where sand comes from and how it is formed. The weather offers many opportunities for discussion—why rain falls, how puddles dry up on a sunny day, how the wind feels and what it does when it blows.

The teacher may introduce ecological ideas around three central themes: (1) the overuse of natural resources (cutting down forests, depleting fossil fuels), (2) the destruction of natural resources (damming up rivers, killing off of species), and (3) the pollution of air and water (by chemicals, industrial wastes, auto exhaust, littering).

The teacher can help increase a child's awareness of man's dependence on the environment as well as man's ability to destroy it. Active involvement in experiences related to the child—littering, for example—can provide experiences stressing the importance of individual responsibility for maintaining the balance of nature.

An annotated list of ecology books for children and for teachers is included at the end of this section.

The inside area has many places for discovery to occur—the

> 1. *Refer to the Bibliography of Resources at the end of this section for books to display in the science area.*
> 2. *Write to publishers for additional materials (Thomas Y. Crowell, New York, is especially good for children's books on science).*
> 3. *Display large posters of subjects relating to the science project.*
> 4. *Take Polaroid pictures of the children engaged in science activities and display them.*
> 5. *Tape-record interesting facts about the science project and provide a playback machine for the children to operate. The "play" and "reverse" buttons can be color-coded.*
> 6. *Cover the holes in a Hallowe'en eye mask to use with children in tasks which call for them to close their eyes.*

principle of balance while building with blocks or while walking on high heels in the playhouse, resonance and tone changes while listening to the piano, autoharp, or guitar, why the teacher washes an open scrape or cut with soap and water, why popcorn pops, or where jello goes when it dissolves (see Part Five: Cooking). Some of the teacher's best times for teaching will be spontaneous.

The activities selected and devised for this section are oriented toward the kind of concepts and mental operations which the young child is capable of handling. Many science experiments currently on the market and presumably designed for the preschooler are far too complex. They may be fun and exciting and the child may even repeat the words, but it is important to present activities which give him the information and first-hand experience necessary for internalization of logical scientific findings.

Below are some suggestions for teaching science activities; it is the teaching strategies you use more than any particular project that determine the quality of a science program in the classroom:

1. Give children plenty of opportunity to explore and experiment on their own.
2. Provide enticing materials which will encourage experimentation.
3. Do not give answers too readily. Instead, ask questions which will stimulate thinking. Try to discover *what* the child is thinking.
4. Ask questions which will encourage children to
   a. hypothesize—"What do you think will happen if we drop the balsa wood into the water? What do you think will happen if we drop the clay into the water?"
   b. identify the result—"What happened?"
   c. predict—"What will happen if we do this again?"
   d. explore other possibilities— "What other things will sink? (float?) (The child should not be expected to understand the concept of specific gravity. Some children will con-

tinue to predict that large objects will sink and small ones float, despite demonstrations that there are exceptions.)

The young child will learn best when information is given in response to his own questions.

Science Activities

Sensory Perception

#1

PROBLEM   *How do different things smell?*

Materials   Baby food jars
Cloves, mint, flower petals, sawdust, leather, onions, apples, etc.

Procedure   1. Place one ingredient in each jar.
2. Punch holes in the lids.
3. Ask children to close their eyes and take turns smelling each jar.
4. Have them guess what they smell.

Conclusion   Different things smell different.

Sensory Perception

#2

PROBLEM   *What sounds do different things make?*

Materials   Common objects in the room

Procedure   1. Have children close their eyes.
2. Produce various sounds such as piece of chalk rubbing on blackboard, pencil dropping on floor, opening and shutting a door, closing a window, turning on a faucet, etc.
3. Ask the children to guess the source of each sound.
4. Ask children to describe how each sound was made.
5. Stress accuracy in description as well as perception.

Conclusion   Different things make different sounds.

Sensory Perception

#3

PROBLEM   *How do different things feel?*

Materials	Objects differing in texture and hardness, such as foam rubber, cork, pennies, velvet, satin, burlap, eraser, marshmallow, etc.
Procedure	1. Let children see all the objects. 2. Have them close their eyes. 3. Have teacher or another child hand them one object at a time to feel. 4. Have children guess what object they are holding.
Conclusion	Different things feel different.
Variation	Place several objects in a bag or box. Have the child put his hand in, select, describe, and guess what the object is before he pulls it out.

Sensory Perception

#4

Problem	*How do different things taste?*
Materials	Variety of common foods, such as apples, popcorn, bread, dry cereal, peanut butter, etc.
Procedure	1. Have children close their eyes. 2. Put a small amount of food in each child's mouth. 3. Have him guess what he is tasting. 4. Have child hold his nose as well as close his eyes. 5. Place food in his mouth and have him guess what he is tasting.
Conclusions	1. Different things taste different. 2. Smelling something helps to tell how it tastes.

Sensory Perception

#5

Problem	*What are some things you can tell with your eyes?*
Materials	Objects which feel the same but look different, such as different colored apples, crayons, or cups; paper with and without pictures or printing, etc.
Procedure	1. Have children close their eyes. 2. Let each one hold an object and tell what he thinks it is. 3. Have him describe all the properties of the object without looking. 4. Ask him questions about each object such as: Is it rough or smooth? Is it hard or soft?

1. Supervise and plan experiments carefully.
2. Repeat experiments and help children to ask questions and arrive at answers for themselves.
3. Keep small sorting objects in designated places and set limits for their use.
4. Do not put out materials without adequate supervision.

Is it round or flat?
What color is it?
Is there a design on it?

Conclusions
1. Your eyes can tell you about the color of things.
2. Your eyes can tell you if things have designs or printing or pictures on them.

Classifying Objects by Their Properties

PROBLEM
In what ways are things alike and different?

Materials
Three cigar boxes
Contac paper
Assortment of buttons, large variety of objects of different shapes and materials, such as marbles, dice, erasers, bolts, bottle caps, coins, spools, plastic objects, pieces of cloth, paper clips, etc.

Procedure
1. Cover cigar boxes with Contac paper.
2. Draw buttons on lid of one box and fill with buttons.
3. Draw pictures of objects with round, triangular, square, and rectangular shapes on another box.
4. Draw pictures of objects made of different kinds of materials on the last box.
5. Fill each box with appropriate objects for sorting.
6. Have child sort according to size, shape, color, texture, materials from which each is made (metal, plastic, wood, cloth).

Conclusion
Things are alike and different because of their color, shape, size, the way they feel, and the things they are made from.

Air Experiment

PROBLEM
What is air? How do you know it's there?

Materials
Bowl of water
Empty glass
Tissue or napkin

Procedure
1. Turn the glass upside down and force it straight down into the bowl of water.

Observation	The glass did not fill up with water.
	2. Tilt the glass to one side.
Observation	There are bubbles that rise and break at the water's surface. These bubbles show that the glass was full of air.
	3. Take the napkin and crumple it up. Place it in the bottom of a clean, dry glass.
	4. Force the glass straight down into the bowl of water and then lift it straight out again.
Observation	The napkin is dry.
	5. Now force the glass straight down into the water and then tilt the glass to one side.
Observation	Water enters the glass and wets the napkin.
Conclusion	Air takes up space even though we can't see it or taste it.
Variations	There are other similar experiments that will show us that air is present all around us: 1. Blowing bubbles 2. Blowing up a balloon 3. Feeling the wind blowing against you 4. Watching all the things the wind blows (smoke, clouds, trees, clothes, kites, flags or banners, pinwheels, curtains, etc.) 5. Using an air pump for bicycle or car tires

Air Pressure Experiment

Problem	*What can air do?*
Materials	Book Balloon
Procedure	1. Place balloon under book. 2. Inflate the balloon.
Observation	The book is rising.
Conclusions	1. Air can lift things up. 2. Air can push things.

Evaporation Experiment

Problem	*How does water get into the air?*
Material	Dish of water
Procedure	1. Place dish of water in the sun.

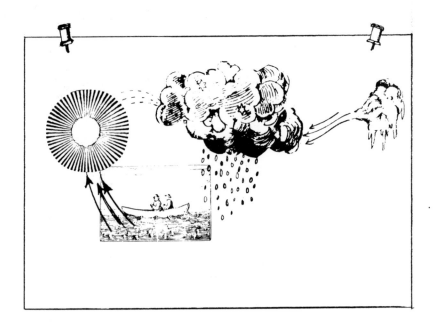

2. After a few hours, check to see what has happened to the water.

Observation   The water is gone.

Conclusions   1. The sun heats the water.
2. The water evaporates and goes into the air.
3. Water from the oceans, rivers, lakes rises into the air when the sun heats it.

Rain Experiment

PROBLEM   *Why does it rain? How can we make rain?*

Materials   Saucepan partially filled with boiling water
Lid of the pan or a plate

Procedure   1. Keep the water boiling in the saucepan and take the lid or the plate and hold it over the pan, but not on it.

Observation   First a thin film of steam covers the plate or lid, and when more steam comes tiny drops of water form on the lid and fall back into the pan.

Conclusion   When water is heated it evaporates and becomes steam. When it is cooled it condenses and becomes water again. The water droplets are like rain that falls. This is just how we get rain. There are lots of tiny drops of water that make a cloud. When these drops are cooled and get too heavy, they have to fall to the ground, and we get rain.

Lightning Experiment

PROBLEM   *What makes lightning?*

> 1. *Type out instructions about how to present tasks and experiments so that volunteers can supervise an activity.*
> 2. *Post interesting facts about animals and science displays so that adults can read them to the children.*
> 3. *Save plastic six-pack drink holders, Mason jar lids, funnels, etc., to use for blowing bubbles.*
> 4. *A teaspoon of glycerin added to water and detergent will make bigger, better bubbles. Blowing bubbles is a good activity for restless children and provides opportunities to talk about rainbows and air.*

Materials   Two long inflated balloons
A darkened room or closet

Procedure   1. Rub the two balloons on your clothes, a rug, or draperies. Hold each end, one to the other, almost touching.

Observation   If the room is dark enough, a spark will jump between the two balloons. That spark is "electricity."

Conclusion   Sparks result from friction. If the balloons had been clouds, the sparks would have been lightning. Lightning is electricity we see in the sky.

Thunder Experiment

PROBLEM   *What makes thunder?*

Material   Empty paper bag

Procedure   1. Blow up paper bag and hold neck tightly so air cannot escape.
2. Hit the bag with the other hand.

Conclusion   The bag will break with a loud bang.

Observation   When air rushes together it makes a loud noise. Lightning forces air apart, and when the air rushes together again it makes a loud noise. Whenever there is lightning forcing the air apart, you will then hear thunder as the air rushes back together.

Rainbow Experiment

PROBLEM   *What makes a rainbow?*

Materials   Garden hose
Small mirror
Glass of water

Procedure	1. Turn the hose on to a fine spray. Stand with your back to the sun.
Observation	You will see a rainbow in the fine spray of water.
	2. Place a small mirror in a glass of water. Place the glass so sun can shine on the mirror. Turn the glass until the rainbow is reflected against the wall or ceiling.
Observation	Look around on the walls or ceiling to find colors of the rainbow.
Conclusion	The sun is made up of all the colors in the rainbow mixed up together. When sunlight hits raindrops or water, the colors are separated.

Note: This conclusion is often too complex for the very young child to understand. If he is at the pre-operational stage his response might be "Oh, that's magic; let me see you do that again!" or "Let me do it." The teacher should encourage this interest and excitement by letting the child "make" his own rainbow. She can help develop an attitude of "things happen for reasons" and "we can look for answers." Arriving at the "correct" conclusion is not always the only objective in an experiment.

Gravity Experiment

PROBLEM	*What is gravity?*
Material	Any object which can be dropped
Procedure	1. Give each child an object and have him drop it. Where does it go?
Observation	It falls to the floor.
	2. Have each child repeat this several times. Each time the child drops the object ask a question such as "Will it fall to the ground this time?" "Will it fall up?" "Will it fall to the side?" "What will happen the next time you drop it?" "What do you think will happen every time you drop it?"
Observation	The object falls to the floor every time. You can predict that the next time you drop the object, it will fall to the floor.
Conclusion	There is a force which pulls everything downward to the center of the earth. This force is called gravity.

Note: Young children will have difficulty understanding or explaining gravity. They will be able to predict that something will fall to the ground based on their experiences but if you ask them "Why?" they are likely to answer "Just because I know it will." It is sufficient to focus on consciously recognizing that objects will fall to the ground every time and that this is predictable.

Learning About Living Things

ANIMALS #1

PROBLEM | *Where do animals come from?*

Materials | Guinea pigs,[1] rabbits, hamsters, rats, kittens

Procedure | 1. Let children care for animals.

Observation | Watch as the female becomes pregnant and bears her litter.

Conclusions | Explain that each of this type of animal (and also people) grow inside the mother. The father plants a seed inside the mother

---

[1] See L. Meshover and S. Feistel (with photographs by E. Hoffmann), *The Guinea Pigs that Went to School* (Chicago: Follett Publishing Company, 1968). This book shows a classroom of children learning about and caring for some guinea pigs and their babies.

AN ACTIVITIES HANDBOOK FOR TEACHERS OF YOUNG CHILDREN

> 1. Sprinkle grass or bird seed on a damp sponge or a scooped-out potato.
> 2. See Bibliography for good books to use to reinforce science concepts.
> 3. Introduce children to simple concepts about the balance of nature, ecology, and conservation.

and the baby grows from this seed. Every animal has both a mother and father.

Discussion   Some animals need to be cared for when they are first born. When you were a baby you could not walk or talk or feed yourself. Your mother and father had to take care of you. Other animals like guinea pigs and kittens and rats and dogs also need someone to take care of them. Some babies like the bees have many worker bees to care for them. The queen bee lays the eggs but she does not take care of the babies.

Learning About Living Things

ANIMALS #2

PROBLEM   *Where do animals come from?*

Materials   Chickens, snakes, spiders, ducks, turtles

Procedure   1. Let children care for animals and insects.[2]
2. Watch when eggs are laid and hatched.

Observation   Some living things are hatched from eggs laid by the mother.

Discussion   Different types of living things are born in different ways. All chicks are born the same way; all snakes are born the same way; all humans are born the same way. Some babies, such as turtles, frogs, fish, and most insects, have to take care of themselves as soon as they hatch. The seahorse is a good example of one of the different ways living things are born. The female gives her eggs to the male and he carries them until the babies are born.

The teacher might use this opportunity to explore social and physical concepts with questions such as:

Could an elephant have a baby dog?

Can boys have babies?

Were your parents once babies?

Do your mom and dad have a mommy and daddy?

Is an animal a living thing? a plant? a rock?

---

[2] See S. S. Greenberg and E. L. Raskin, *Home-Made Zoo* (New York: David McKay Company, 1952). Listed in annotated bibliography at the end of this part, page 84.

Learning About Living Things

ANIMALS #3

PROBLEM

How do tadpoles turn into frogs?

Materials

Terrarium
Frog eggs from stream, pond, or lake
Plenty of pond water and some of the plants

Procedure

1. Put frog eggs, pond water, and plants in the terrarium and watch daily for tadpoles to hatch.

Observation

Soon tadpoles or pollywogs will hatch.

2. Boiled spinach or other leafy vegetables and the yolk of a hard boiled egg can be added for extra food supply for the growing tadpoles.

Observation

The hind legs will begin to grow first, then the front legs. The tail gets smaller and lungs will replace the gills.

3. Large rocks and dry areas will need to be provided in the terrarium as the frogs develop, or they can be returned to their natural environment.

Observation

Grown frogs like to eat bugs, spiders, worms, and insects.

Conclusion

Some animals don't look like their parents when they are born. Tadpoles do not look like frogs when they are born, but they grow into frogs.

Suggestion

Use Leo Lionni's book *Fish Is Fish,* New York: Pantheon, 1970.

Learning About Living Things

PLANTS #1

PROBLEM

How do different plants grow?

Materials

Assorted seeds: radish, carrot, corn, bell pepper, tomato, flower seeds
Glass jars
Blotter paper, cotton, or paper towels

Procedure

1. Sandwich the seeds between the blotter paper or towels and the inside of the glass jar.
2. Pour enough water in the jar to soak up into the blotter. Keep in sunny place.

Observation

Soon the seeds will grow. Watch the roots grow downward toward the water and the stems upward toward the sunlight.

3. Seedlings may be transferred to soil cups or into the ground.

Observation

Plants take food from the soil and need space to grow.

Conclusion

Some plants grow from seeds. The wind, water, and insects and animals carry seeds to new and different places for them to grow into more plants.

Learning About Living Things

PLANTS #2

PROBLEM

How do plants get their food?

Materials

Growing plants
Celery stalks
Red food coloring

Procedure

1. Put a celery stalk into a glass of colored water.

Observation

In a few hours the leaves turn red.

2. Cut across the stem of the celery stalk.

Observation

The red spots are the veins which carried the water up to the leaves.

3. Observe the root system of other growing plants.

Observation

Plants carry food from the ground up through the roots and veins.

HELPFUL HINTS

> 1. *Collect shells, fossils, and rocks on a nature walk.*
> 2. *Ask parents to bring their collections of science materials to share.*
> 3. *Encourage girls as well as boys to participate in science activities.*
> 4. *Save old clocks, radios, motors, etc., to take apart.*

Conclusion

Plants can make their own food with the help of the sun and water and minerals from the soil.

Suggestion

Collect and identify leaves common to the immediate environment. Discuss the fact that leaves are necessary to plants because they take water and minerals from the soil, gases from the air and with the help of sunlight, the leaves manufacture food for the plant. When the food is stored, such as in nuts and seeds, the leaves drop off because they are no longer needed. Food is stored in various parts of plants: leaves (lettuce, spinach, cabbage), stems (asparagus, celery, green onions), underground stems (onions, potatoes), roots (beets, carrots, radishes, sweet potatoes), flowers (artichokes, broccoli, cauliflower), fruits (apples, pears, tomatoes, peaches, plums, apricots), and seeds (nuts, peas, beans).

Learning About Living Things

PLANTS #3

PROBLEM

Do all plants grow from seeds?

Materials

Carrot tops
Sweet potatoes
Onions
Flower cuttings such as geraniums

Procedure

1. Place the sweet potato in a jar of water.
2. Place the carrot top with leaves removed in a dish of water.
3. Place onion in a jar of water.
4. Put flower cuttings in glass of water.

Observation

New plants will begin to grow.

Conclusion

Some plants do not need seeds to grow.

Learning About Living Things

SPORES AND MOLDS

PROBLEM

Do all plants grow from seeds?

Materials	A large jar Piece of bread
Procedure	1. Expose a piece of bread to the air overnight. 2. Put the bread in a closed jar. 3. Make sure the bread is kept moist.
Observation	Soon a bread mold will start to grow—blue, grey, and green in color.
	4. Turn the bread upside down and gently tap it.
Observation	The spores will fall off.
Conclusion	Plants such as yeast, mushrooms, ferns, lichens, and molds grow from spores. Most spores do not form new plants.

Learning About Living Things

CHEMICAL GROWTH EXPERIMENT

PROBLEM	*Can chemicals grow?*
Materials	Glass bowl or plate (no metal) Broken pieces of brick or charcoal briquets Porous rocks Pieces of sponge or synthetic foam rubber Jar 6 tablespoons water 6 tablespoons salt (3 for solution, 3 for sprinkling) 6 tablespoons laundry bluing 3 tablespoons household ammonia Food coloring—plastic flowers or succulents
Procedure	1. Dampen rocks, briquets, and sponge. 2. Arrange these ingredients in a glass plate or shallow bowl. 3. Mix chemicals in jar, using 3 tablespoons salt. 4. Pour mixture to saturate all the rocks and briquets and sponge to dampen thoroughly. A few drops of food coloring can be dropped on the tops of the high points of the arrangement. Sprinkle remaining 3 tbsp. salt evenly over the display. Add small plastic flowers or succulents to give more of a garden effect.
Observation	In a few hours, a "coral-like" growth of crystals begins to form on the solid materials and the rim of the bowl.
	5. Add more chemicals if some places seem bare. Allow growth to continue for several days.
Observation	Within a day the growth will spread and continue for several days.

Conclusion Chemical growth is made up of complex salts which form as the liquid evaporates. The porous materials soak up the liquid and carry it to the surface where it evaporates, leaving the salts behind. The deposit continues to grow because each of the crystals which has formed is likewise able to carry the liquid through itself and to the surface, leaving even more crystals behind. Growth can be started again by adding a teaspoon or so of ammonia.

Bibliography of Resources

Books About Science for the Teacher

Brandwein, Paul F., and Elizabeth K. Cooper. *Concepts in science.* New York: Harcourt, Brace & World, 1967. An illustrated book without text, showing scenes such as children playing with magnets and levers, chicks hatching, etc. Sections cover investigating matter, investigating force, investigating plants and animals. Another section shows pictures of children from different ethnic groups and there is also a page of living and non-living things. A list of science words is supplied at the end of the book.

Carmichael, Viola. *Science experiences for young children.* Los Angeles: Southern California Association for the Education of Young Children, 1969. Sections of this book are devoted to plants, animals, weather, human body, cooking, machines, developing concepts, etc. Each section provides the teacher with background information, suggested class projects, art and craft ideas, and book lists.

Gale, Frank C., and Clarice W. Gale. *Experiences with plants for young children.* Palo Alto, Ca.: Pacific Books, 1974. A resource book for use primarily with four- and five-year-olds. Two categories of experiences are provided. In the first, entitled "Exploring," the observational power of the child is sharpened, but no comparison of materials is made. In the second, "Exploring, Comparing, and Seeing Relationships," the child is asked to make comparisons between two or more objects, events, or ideas. He is given opportunities to make simple measurements, use properly-explained controls in experimenting, count, and note cause-and-effect and simple space and time relationships.

Greenberg, Sylvia S., and Edith L. Raskin. *Home-made zoo.* David McKay, 1952. Teachers and parents will find this book a useful guide in caring for small animals such as hamsters, rabbits, mice, guinea pigs, birds, turtles, fish, etc. The authors provide helpful information on the buying of pets, how to build cages, sanitation, feeding, and some of the common ailments.

Haupt, Dorothy. *Science experiences for nursery school children.* Washington, D.C.: National Association for the Education of Young Children. This booklet offers a discussion of the teacher's role in providing science experiences in the nursery school with some examples and a list of resource materials.

Kranzer, Herman C. *Nature and science activities for young children.* Jenkintown, Pa.: Baker, 1969. A booklet of activities grouped according to such subjects as plants, animals, weather, light, time, tools, and machines. Each page provides ideas for a display, an activity, or experiment, with suggestions to the teacher on how she can extend these learnings in the classroom.

McGavack, John Jr., and Donald P. LaSalle. *Guppies, bubbles, and vibrating objects.* New York: John Day, 1969. The subtitle of this book is "A creative approach to the teaching of science to very young children," and the book lives up to its title very successfully. The authors emphasize student involvement with simple, carefully designed activities to help young children develop healthy attitudes and to increase their curiosity through active exploration. An excellent resource book.

Morris, Loverne. *Frogs as wild pets.* Chicago: Children's Press, 1973. A useful resource of scientific information about different kinds of frogs; how to find, capture, feed, and tame them. Includes a glossary of scientific terms. Illustrations by Arnold Mesches.

Notkin, Jerome J., and Sidney Gulkin. *The how and why wonder book of beginning science.* Columbus, Ohio: Charles E. Merrill, 1960. A basic science book with concepts suitable for the teacher and parent to read as background information. The ideas can be adapted for use at a much simpler level with the preschooler. Some of the experiments suggested include "How Can You Bend Light?" "How Can You Burn Paper Without a Match?" "How Do Jet Planes Work?" and "Do Green Plants Need Air?"

Piltz, Albert, *et al. Discovering science, a readiness book.* Columbus, Ohio: Charles E. Merrill, 1968. Large pictures and illustrations are presented with only a word or short sentence accompanying each picture. Contents include a section on "Finding Out," showing pictures of children using their five senses to explore materials (children blindfolded touching objects, tasting, smelling, etc.). Other sections include pictures about sound, magnets, gravity, weather, seasons, animals, and plants. Pictures are good for discussion. Some of the simple questions can lead to clarification of what the child needs to know in order to have a basis for clearer understanding of a concept.

Rieger, Edythe. *Science adventures in children's play.* New York: The Play Schools Association, 1968. This is a booklet written for teachers of elementary school science, but the preschool teacher will find it useful as a resource for ideas to incorporate into her curriculum. There are helpful suggestions and background information on such topics as exploring the neighborhood, insects, collections, and ideas for program enrichment. Bibliography of resource books also.

Selsam, Millicent E. *Animals as parents.* New York: William Morrow, 1965. This is a good book for the teacher and parent to have as a resource for background information. The topics include birds and mammals as parents and provide much interesting information, such as the fact that birds lay certain numbers of eggs. The catbird usually lays four; pigeons lay two while a duck lays up to sixteen. There is also a simply written and interesting section about mother love among monkeys and apes and the role of early experience. The author has also written other books about plants and animals, all worth having in the teacher's library. Nicely illustrated by John Kaufmann.

Victor, Edward. *Science for the elementary school.* Toronto: Macmillan, Collier-Macmillan Canada, Ltd., 1970. Although this book was written for the elementary grades, the preschool teacher ought to use it as a resource for some of the most up-to-date information available on science programs. The author discusses objectives and methods of teaching science and provides sample lessons. Much of this basic information can be adapted for use in the nursery school, or it can be used simply as background material for the teacher who wishes to be better informed about science. There is a valuable section of references and free and inexpensive materials; also included are places to write for information, journals, magazines, bulletins, sourcebooks of experiments and demonstrations, science series, films and filmstrips. Well worth looking at, even if you don't buy it.

Vivian, Charles. *Science experiments & amusements for children.* New York: Dover, 1963. This booklet contains seventy-three simple experiments which the young child can do. However, as with most activity books in science, the teacher of pre-schoolers must remember that the child may not grasp the concept of why certain things happen. For example, some of the activities demonstrate how hot water rises, or how air presses in all directions. The child may not understand why this happens, but it may still be useful to let him try some of these simpler activities so he can have first-hand experiences in watching what does happen.

Wyler, Rose. *Question and answer adventures, science.* New York: Golden Press, 1965. A simple resource book for the teacher to provide ideas which she can incorporate into the science curriculum of the preschool. Forty-five experiments and activities include growing spores, plants that make seeds, light and shadow, animal babies, what is inside the earth, the solar system.

Some useful references for the teacher:

Ranger Rick's nature magazine, published by the National Wildlife Federation, 1412 16th St., N.W., Washington, D.C. 20036. This magazine presents simply written and informative articles about wildlife. The lovely photographs in every issue make this a particularly valuable resource for the teacher.

Science books, A Quarterly Review, published by the American Association for the Advancement of Science, 1515 Massachusetts Ave., N.W., Washington, D.C. 20005. Short reviews and recommendations for all science publications. Annotations include listings for various age groups including kindergarten and preschool. Useful, timesaving resource for the teacher.

Books About Science for Children

Arneson, D. J. *Secret places.* New York: Holt, Rinehart, & Winston, 1971. Beautiful vivid photographs of a young boy's secret places in the countryside around his home. He takes the reader on a tour and expresses the hope that "progress"—machines and construction— will never find his secret places. Good feeling for the preservation of natural open spaces. Photos by Peter Arnold.

Baer, Edith. *The wonder of hands.* New York: Parents' Magazine Press, 1970. The text, accompanied by Tana Hoban's sensitive photography, portrays the many ways hands communicate; hands can heal, plant a seed, finger-paint, wave goodby.

Bartlett, Margaret Farrington. *The clean brook.* New York: Thomas Y. Crowell, 1960. The story of the changing life of a brook, how the natural water filters the various sediment, and the various animals that frequent it. Clear, realistic illustrations by Alden A. Watson. Good book to introduce the children to natural environment. Look for other books from the "Let's Read and Find Out" science series.

Branley, Franklyn. *What makes day and night.* New York: Thomas Y. Crowell, 1961. A simple, detailed explanation describing the mechanics of the earth's rotation.

Brenner, Barbara. *Faces.* New York: E. P. Dutton, 1970. Photos and script about the senses stemming from the face—eyes, ears, nose, mouth. Simple, concise text. Photos by George Ancona show how you use each of the senses, illustrates how every face is different but has some things in common. Good to use in conjunction with body parts and exploration of the senses.

Carle, Eric. *The very hungry caterpillar.* New York: World, 1971. A simple and colorful book to use in showing stages of growth in a caterpillar. There are holes in the bright illustrations of leaves and fruit showing what the caterpillar consumes as it grows.

Collier, Ethel. *Who goes there in my garden?* New York: Young Scott Books, 1963. With his birthday money, a boy buys seeds to plant a spring garden. Discusses planting, garden insects. A good book to read to children before planting a garden.

Gans, Roma. *It's nesting time.* New York: Thomas Y. Crowell, 1964. An informative and highly educational book designed to teach young children to observe and respect the nests of various birds. Illustrations by Mizumura show how different birds build their nests with different kinds of materials and designs.

Gans, Roma, and Franklyn M. Branley (eds.). *Let's-read-and-find-out science books.* New York: Thomas Y. Crowell. This is a very well planned series of books designed for children on such topics as *Air is all around you, How a seed grows, What makes a shadow?* and *Your skin and mine.*

One of the series, *My hands* (by Aliki, 1962), describes the fingers and thumb, how hands are necessary for work and expression and gets the child to think about his own hands. The concepts are written for the young child and the easy-to-read text is colorfully illustrated. *My five senses* is another written by the same author.

Find out by touching (by Paul Showers, 1961), suggests to the child that he feel common objects such as the book, a window, the carpet, and learn how his sense of touch can tell him many things about the world around him. Through touch, the child learns about the concepts of hard, soft, smooth, rough, cold, warm, etc.

Garelick, May. *Where does the butterfly go when it rains?* New York: Young Scott Books, 1961. Story concerns the "mystery" of where the butterfly goes when it rains. The author shows what happens to other creatures—the bee flies back to its hive, water slides off a duck's back, etc. Encourages the child to look and discover the answers for himself. Blue-hued illustrations give the impression of rain.

Goldreich, Gloria, and Esther Goldreich. *What can she be? a veterinarian.* New York: Lothrop, Lee & Shepard, 1972. Children who have had to take a pet to the veterinarian will appreciate the photographs (by Robert Ipcar) showing a typical day in the life of a woman vet caring for injured and sick puppies, cats, and bunnies.

Hawes, Judy. *What I like about toads.* New York: Thomas Y. Crowell, 1969. "I didn't used to like toads. I thought toads gave me warts."

The author helps children see the usefulness of toads and their habits.

Krauss, Ruth. *The carrot seed.* New York: Harper & Brothers, 1945. There are some things little children just know, that's all. And even when everyone said it wouldn't come up, the little boy knew his very own carrot seed would grow.

Leaf, Munro. *Who cares? I do.* New York: J. B. Lippincott, 1971. Cartoon-like figures alongside photographs supplied by the U.S. Forest Service, The National Park Service, and Keep America Beautiful, Inc., help the child to see that "our country is getting to be a mess. And we seem to be the best ones to do something about it."

Leen, Nina. *And then there were none.* New York: Holt, Rinehart & Winston, 1973. Over 100 species of wildlife in the United States are endangered, and prizewinning photographer Nina Leen has presented more than 50 of these rare animals in a book well worth having for children to see. Commentaries by zoologist Joseph A. Davis explain the causes of endangerment.

Lionni, Leo. *Fish is fish.* New York: Pantheon Books, 1970. "The minnow and the tadpole were inseparable friends. . . ." But the tadpole grows up and becomes a frog and goes off to explore the world. He returns to tell his friend about the extraordinary things he has seen and convinces Fish he too should venture out of the pond. Humorous sketches of Fish's dreams. A good book to use with tadpoles and fish in a science project.

Lowery, Lawrence F., and Evelyn Moore. *I wonder why readers.* New York: Holt, Rinehart & Winston, 1969. A series of 24 books designed for early grades but useful for preschool. They cover general topics of language arts, and science activities. *Quiet as a butterfly* stresses listening as an observational skill. It suggests that the teacher ask the class to think of things that make a sound and to finish stories with starting lines like "If I were a yellow butterfly, I would. . . ." The series contains such titles as *Soft as a bunny, Look and see, Up, up in a balloon, What does an animal eat,* and *Larry's racing machine.* The accompanying teacher's guide is valuable for ideas and suggestions as to how these books can be used for language and science. Can be easily adapted for use in the preschool. Well illustrated in color with sturdy covers.

Mallinson, George G., *et al. Science 1.* Morristown, N.J.: Silver Burdett, 1965. Excellent color photos which encourage discussion. Some portions may be too sophisticated, but most cover topics which the preschooler can discuss, such as "Plant Life on the Earth," "You and Your Body," "The Sounds You Hear," "How Work is Done" ("Some things are too big to push and pull. Your muscles are not strong enough. Big machines help do the work.").

Mari, Iela, and Enzo Mari. *The apple and the moth.* New York: Dial Press, 1970. Lovely picture book about the metamorphosis of a moth and its stages—egg on leaf, caterpillar, cocoon, moth. All occur in one apple tree. Teacher and children can make up their own descriptions to accompany the drawings. A book without words which tells its own story. Use with display of caterpillars and cocoons.

————. *The chicken and the egg.* New York: Pantheon Books, 1969. A hen lays an egg and the following sequence of pictures shows the development of the chick until it finally hatches. Can be used in studying growth cycles.

Podendorf, Illa. *The true book of science experiments.* Chicago: Children's Press, 1972. Experiments for the young child about gravity, magnets, air, water, sound, heat, and cold.

Selsam, Millicent E. *Is this a baby dinosaur?* New York: Harper & Row, 1972. Photographs stress the importance of careful observation. With a photograph of lentil seeds, for example, the caption asks "Are these pebbles?" This author produces consistently excellent books on science for the young child.

Shuttlesworth, Dorothy E. *Clean air—sparkling water; the fight against pollution.* New York: Doubleday, 1968. "We can live without many things. But not without air. Not without water. And the air must be clean. The water must be pure." A series of photographs with a text designed for the older reader helps tell the story of pollution and how man can fight back. The teacher can read the captions of the pictures to young children and underline the simpler concepts in the text.

Stone, A. Harris. *The last free bird.* Englewood Cliffs, N.J.: Prentice-Hall, 1967. Lovely watercolor illustrations by Sheila Heins enhance a very simple text which tells of man's destruction of the nesting and feeding places of birds.

Tresselt, Alvin. *The dead tree.* New York: Parents' Magazine Press, 1972. The reader is helped to appreciate the natural cycle of life in the forest where even a dead tree serves to enhance new growth. A good book for ecology.

Udry, Janice May. *A tree is nice.* New York: Harper & Row, 1956. An old favorite showing why trees are nice to have around. You can climb on them, eat their fruit, hang a swing, picnic in their shade, and plant your very own. Encourages observation of nature.

Part 3 / **Exploring the Arts**

Introduction

The young child spends a large part of his day in activities which concern the affective areas of his life—the visual and tactile arts, music, dance, storytelling and dramatic play. Yet many programs of early education convey the attitude through their curricula that these activities are unimportant or merely "frills."

When compared with cognitively oriented tasks such as pre-math and science, children's learning in the arts is more difficult to measure and specify. Because of the stress on teaching formal skills, and because goals in such activities as painting, working with play dough, dancing, and dramatic play are not easily articulated and measured, the arts are often relegated to a position of relative unimportance.

Some teachers believe that the arts should be child-oriented and deal with processes, not products. This approach is still valid. The child learns best about the arts if they are a natural part of his life, that is, if he hears all kinds of music during the day, if he sees and touches a variety of art and art materials, and if he is provided with many opportunities to investigate and experience different ways of expressing his feelings and ideas. However, including the arts as a natural part of the total curriculum rather than setting aside periods for formal instruction does not preclude the teacher's having certain objectives in mind. The teacher may want to let one of the children pound the play dough as hard as he can to work off some of his angry feelings; another time, she may use the play dough to teach conservation of quantity. Both are effective ways to use the arts.

The activities within Part Three were designed to help the teacher specify objectives more clearly. (See Hess/Croft text, *Teachers of Young Children,* Chapter 14.) They are not intended

> *1. Use art recipes to introduce children to the metric system.*
> *2. Order metric chart (C 13.10; 304) from Supt. of Documents, U.S. Government Printing Office, Washington, D.C. 20402 (55¢).*
> *3. Purchase scales, dry and liquid measuring containers, and have children help translate measurements from recipes (see play dough).*
> *4. Practice use of terms in the metric system.*
> *5. For more information, write to: Metric Information Office, National Bureau of Standards, Washington, D.C. 20234*

as formal teaching tasks, but should be adapted to suit the needs of the children.

Some of the music activities were designed to teach the child about the rate of speed (tempo), accent on beats (rhythm), differentiation between high and low tones, meaning of lyrics (text), and emotional impact of music (mood). The recommended records accompanying some of these tasks were suggested by teachers who have found them especially useful, but these basics can be taught with any number of other songs and records. Initially, it is helpful to use material which is familiar to the young child, those songs which are part of his life style. Gradually, the child's musical exposure can be increased to include selections from other cultures, action songs, story songs, classical, country, popular, soul music, jazz, opera, etc.

Experiences in sound discrimination are also included in the auditory perception section of Part One.

The sensorimotor exploration and the creative movement activity are two very different approaches to movement. The former is concerned primarily with gross motor experiences in order to help the child develop strength and coordination. Through these exercises the child becomes physically aware of his own body as well as of space and directionality (useful in remembering letter forms and achieving a left-right orientation). Comprehension of form, line, and space are fundamentals in art and architecture. Though not conclusive, research indicates that there is some evidence that a correlation does exist between sensorimotor skills and reading and writing readiness.

The creative movement activities are designed to promote self-discovery—an appreciation of the individual's uniqueness. Physical expression and interpretation of inner feelings lead to greater self-awareness and a healthier self-concept. Thus the teacher should use the suggested activities and records within a loose framework which provides her with the opportunity to respond sensitively and flexibly to each child.

Each of the sections within Part Three is accompanied by an annotated list of resource materials and places to write for more information. The role of the teacher in the arts is to encourage self-discovery in both the affective and cognitive areas. This will be best achieved if she has specific objectives in mind, has a large repertoire of effective resource materials and tasks, and presents these materials not rigidly, but with an awareness based on knowledge of the child's learning process.

Art Recipes

Visual and Tactile Experiences

Introduction

Paints may be mixed with different ingredients to suit different needs. Generally speaking, an *extender* is used to cut down the cost of paints and to give the desired consistency; it can also be added to tempera to make finger paint. Soap (not detergent) is added to make paint easier to wash out as well as to help it adhere to slick surfaces, such as glass or cellophane. Detergent is added to prevent cracking when paints dry. Alum may be added as a preservative, and a few drops of glycerin or oil of wintergreen will keep paint mixture fresh. Condensed milk gives a glossy effect. Following are some basic recipes for extender, easel paint, finger paint, and plastic art materials.

BASIC BENTONITE EXTENDER	*1 cup Bentonite (powered Bentonite may be purchased at most ceramic supply stores)* *½ cup soap powder* *2 quarts water* *Mix well with beater (or preferably in a blender). Let stand in crock or plastic container 2 or 3 days; stir each day. (Do not use metal container.)*
EASEL PAINT/RECIPE #1	*For large quantities of paint, measure 6 to 8 tbsp. extender into large jar. Pour in 1 1-lb. can powdered paint. Stir in 3 cups liquid starch and 2 tbsp. soap flakes. Add water to desired consistency.*
EASEL PAINT/RECIPE #2	*Mix 1 part powdered paint, 2 parts detergent, 2 parts water.*
EASEL PAINT/RECIPE #3	*Mix in blender: 1 1-lb. can powdered paint, ¼ cup liquid starch, about ⅓ to ½ cup water, and 1 large tbsp. soap powder.*
FINGER PAINT/RECIPE #1	*Mix 1 cup laundry starch with 1 cup cold water. (Do not use instant laundry starch.) Add 4 cups boiling water and cook until clear, stirring constantly. (The mixture will not be as thick as the finished product.) Add 1 cup soap flakes and ¼ cup talcum powder (optional). Beat with egg beater until smooth. (This should give the desired consistency.) Store in plastic container in refrigerator.*
FINGER PAINT/RECIPE #2	*Gradually add 2 quarts water to 1 cup corn starch. Cook until clear and add ½ cup soap flakes. A few drops of glycerin or oil of wintergreen may be added.*
FINGER PAINT/RECIPE #3	*Mix 1 cup dry starch with ½ cup water in a container that can take boiling water. Add 1½ cups boiling water and stir rapidly. Add ¾ cups powdered detergent and stir again until smooth.*

HELPFUL HINTS

1. *Provide plenty of elbow room and plenty of time for children to finger-paint.*
2. *Finger-paint on a smooth table top; scrape paint off with spatulas.*
3. *Some children prefer to paint with cold cream on a sheet of oil cloth.*
4. *Finished products are less important than the experience of finger painting.*
5. *Roll up sleeves, put on aprons, show children where to wash up before giving them the finger paints.*
6. *Be sure you have running water and towels nearby, or provide a large basin where children can rinse off.*
7. *Offer finger paints frequently, at different times of the day and in different areas of the school (indoors and out).*
8. *Food coloring or powdered paint may be added to the mixture before using; or, allow the child to choose the colors he wants sprinkled on top of the paint.*
9. *Try using warm finger paints and pastel shades.*
10. *Separate disruptive children and limit the number who can finger-paint at one time.*

FINGER PAINT/RECIPE #4

A mixture of 1 cup laundry starch, 1 cup cold water and 3 cups soap flakes will provide a quick finger paint. (This is more textured than the cooked finger paint.)

FINGER PAINT/RECIPE #5

Add a non-detergent liquid soap to liquid starch to facilitate clean-up. Sprinkle tempera on top of starch as used.

FINGER PAINT/RECIPE #6

Mix in blender: 1 1-lb. can powdered paint, ¼ cup liquid starch, ⅓ to ½ cup water, and 1 tbsp. soap powder.

FINGER PAINT/RECIPE #7

Mix 1 cup flour and 1 cup cold water. Add 3 cups boiling water and bring all to a boil, stirring constantly. Add 1 tbsp. coloring. Paintings from this recipe dry flat and do not need to be ironed.

PLASTIC ART RECIPES

PLAY DOUGH

Mix together 4 cups flour, ¼ cup salt and ¼ cup powdered tempera paint. Gradually add approximately 1½ cups water mixed with 1 tbsp. oil. Keep kneading the mixture as you add the liquid. Add more water if too stiff, more flour if too sticky. Let children help with the mixing and measuring.

Metric measurements for mixing playdough:

AN ACTIVITIES HANDBOOK FOR TEACHERS OF YOUNG CHILDREN

HELPFUL HINTS

1. *Mix large quantities of play dough so that each child can have a big piece to play with.*
2. *Mix two or three different colors, and let the children knead portions together to make new colors.*
3. *Mix white, brown, or black play dough and listen and observe differences in the kind of talk or play that these colors stimulate.*
4. *Provide cooky cutters, rolling pins, plastic pie crust cutters, other utensils; remove these occasionally to encourage more direct contact between the child and the art medium.*
5. *The play dough table and paint easel are good places to start a shy or reluctant child.*
6. *Add liquid food coloring to water before mixing with flour; add powdered tempera to flour before adding water.*

1 cup flour = 125 grams or ⅛ kilogram
¼ cup salt = about 40 grams
1 cup water = ¼ liter; 1½ cups water = ⅜ liter
1 cup water = 375 cc. (cubic centimeters)

MODELING "GOOP"

Stir 2 cups table salt and ⅔ cup water over low to medium heat for 4–5 minutes. Remove from heat. Mix 1 cup corn starch with ½ cup water and add to first mixture. Stir until smooth. Return mixture to low heat and continue to stir. The "goop" will thicken quickly. This may be used for modeling and will not crumble when dry as some clay products tend to do when unfired. Objects like beads and colored macaroni may be added. Store unused portions in a plastic bag or airtight can.

CRAFT CLAY

Combine 1 cup corn starch, 2 cups baking soda (1 lb. box), and 1¼ cups water and cook until thickened to doughlike consistency. Turn mixture out on pastry board and knead. Cover with damp cloth or keep in plastic bag. Good for plaques and other "models" which can be painted when dry.

COOKED PLAY DOUGH

Combine 1 cup flour, ½ cup salt and 2 tsp. cream of tartar in a large saucepan. Gradually stir in 1 cup water mixed with 2 tbsp. oil and 1 tsp. food coloring. Cook over medium to high heat, stirring constantly until a ball forms. Remove from heat and knead until smooth.

COOKED SODA DOUGH

Mix 1 lb. baking soda, 1 lb. cornstarch, and 1¼ cup water. Cook over medium heat until too thick to stir. Knead the mixture as it cools. This modeling mixture has a different consistency from those made with flour. Keeps well in an airtight container, and more water can be added to rework the dough when needed.

HELPFUL HINTS

1. *Display artwork at child's eye level.*
2. *Place art materials on low shelves so children can get their own.*
3. *Encourage independence and cooperation. Have more capable children show less experienced children how to mix paints, find materials, take paintings off easels, help with putting on and taking off aprons, and wiping up.*
4. *Clean-up should be an expected part of any art project.*
5. *Make "picture recipes" and post them near the ingredients and necessary measuring and mixing utensils so that children can make their own paints and play dough.*
6. *Relate art activities to all other parts of the curriculum.*
7. *Avoid using models or asking child what he is making.*
8. *Provide plenty of materials, but discourage waste. Salvage leftover and used art materials and paper for other activities. Cut up scraps for collage.*
9. *Give each child plenty of time to explore an activity. Let a child tell you when he is finished rather than asking him if he is finished. Don't rush a child from one thing to another.*
10. *Provide test tubes in a stand (or small baby-food jars) with water, eyedroppers, and food coloring, so that children can mix primary and secondary colors.*
11. *Read "How to Talk to a Scribbler," by Joseph and Marilyn Sparling (*Young Children*, August, 1973, pp. 333–41).*

BAKED DOUGH

Mix together 4 cups flour, 1 cup salt, and enough water (about 1½–2 cups) to make a stiff dough. Provide materials such as rocks, peas, macaroni, buttons and other scrap materials for children to press into their dough shapes. Bake in slow oven (about 250°) for one hour. For an antiqued effect, brush on condensed milk before baking or a mixture of condensed milk and food coloring.

COLORED SALT PASTE

Mix 2 parts salt to 1 part flour. Add powdered paint and enough water to make a smooth heavy paste. Keep in air tight container.

Variation: *Add small amount of boiling water to regular library paste and stir in colored tempera. This gives collages a lacquered finish.*

CREPE PAPER PASTE

Cut or tear 2 tbsp. crepe paper of a single color. The finer the paper is cut, the smoother the paste will be.
Add ½ tbsp. flour, ½ tbsp. salt, and enough water to make a paste. Stir and squash the mixture until it is as smooth as possible. Store in air tight container.

AN ACTIVITIES HANDBOOK FOR TEACHERS OF YOUNG CHILDREN

SQUEEZE BOTTLE GLITTER | *Mix equal parts of flour, salt, and water. Pour into plastic squeeze bottles such as those used for ketchup. Liquid colored tempera may be added for variety. Squeeze onto heavy construction paper or cardboard. The salt gives the designs a glistening quality when dry.*

Art Activities

Visual and Tactile Experiences

PASTE PAINTING | *Mix 3 tbsp. paste with 2 tbsp. powdered tempera. Stir in about 2 to 3 tbsp. hot water or until mixture is smooth but still quite thick. Provide tongue depressors and heavy cardboard for children to create paintings that have a thick, textured look.*

SPATTER PAINTING | *Cut 6-inch squares of wire screening and frame with colored tape. Place over leaves or other objects on paper and spatter paint with toothbrush.*

COLORED BUBBLES | *Mix 1 cup granulated soap in 1 quart warm water. Add food coloring and mix well. Provide each child with a plastic straw and some of the mix in a juice can.*

STRING PICTURES | *Dip yarn or string in mixture of paint and white glue, then make designs on colored paper.*

BLOW OUT PICTURES | *Dip the end of small tubing, such as plastic straw, cardboard tube, or metal tube into thinned tempera paint. Lift out quickly to sheet of paper. Blow through tubing to create fun pictures. Fold pictures in half while paint is still wet and make interesting Rorschach-like designs.*

PRINTING | *Provide several pie tins of different colored easel paints. Let children "print" by dipping a variety of objects into the paint and making impressions on absorbent paper. Use such printing objects as vegetables, hair curlers, nuts, bolts, kitchen utensils, plastic table toys. Very young children will tend to make a painting or scribbling experience out of this. Kitchen tools with handles, such as mashers and cooky cutters, are good for beginners.*

ROLL PAINTING | *Fill roll-on deodorant bottles with slightly thickened tempera and let children use at the art table for making designs on paper.*

EYE DROPPER PAINTING | *Provide small juice cans or other sturdy containers of slightly*

HELPFUL HINTS

thickened tempera and an assortment of different sized droppers. Let children drop paint onto construction paper to make designs; or simply provide some empty plastic bottles and let children use droppers to mix their own paint colors.

COLORED COLLAGE MATERIALS

Shake rock salt and other porous materials such as egg shells and macaroni in a thin mixture of powder paint or food coloring and alcohol. Use for collage.

COLORED SAND

Mix powdered paint with a fine quality white sand on large sheets of newspaper. Let children squeeze out designs with a mixture of liquid starch and white glue on construction paper. Turn design side down on colored sand.

COLORED CORN MEAL

Mix dry powdered paint with corn meal. Provide children with plastic spoons, small brushes, Q-tips, and small pie tins of white glue, mixed with water or liquid starch. Let children paint on construction paper with the glue. Sprinkle colored corn meal over designs. Shake off excess. A variety of colors can be stored on the shelf to be used at a moment's notice.

FINGER ETCHING

Use masking tape to delineate an area on the surface of a smooth table the same size as colored newsprint you plan to use. Let the child finger-paint on the surface with liquid starch and powdered paint. When he has finished his table-top design, take it off by smoothing newsprint over the design.

BLOTTER ART

Provide water colors or mix powdered tempera and water to a thin consistency. Let children use small paint brushes or eye droppers to make designs on pieces of white blotter paper. Mount the finished product on construction paper of a contrasting color. For an effective display, cover the design with transparent self-sticking shelf paper.

TISSUE COLLAGE

Let children use wide brushes to "paint" liquid starch on cans, carpet yarn spools, construction paper, etc., and apply pieces of colored tissue paper.

FEELING PICTURES

Collect items such as feathers, sequins, dry cereals, textured materials, scrap tiles, pine cones, seed pods, pebbles, shells, buttons,

HELPFUL HINTS

to let children make "feeling" pictures with smooth, rough, glittery, shiny, soft textures.

3-D COLLAGE
Collect items such as pieces of styrofoam, small pieces of wood, soft wood (balsam), string, wire, pipe cleaners, colored macaroni, clothespins, corks, pine cones, nut shells, straws, etc. Give the children some white glue and cellophane tape and let them use their imaginations to make a "creation."

IRONED PICTURES
Let children make design on sheet of wax paper with colored tissue, leaves, other flat pieces of material and scraped bits of old crayons. Cover with similar size wax paper and iron together. Hang so light can shine through.

SEWING CARDS
Cut pieces of cardboard into various shapes. Punch holes about an inch apart around the edges. Stiffen the ends of a string, yarn, or shoelace by wrapping with cellophane tape, or dipping in melted wax. Have the children lace in and out of the holes.

SEWING ON BURLAP
Cut squares of burlap or other loosely woven material into 8 or 10 inch pieces. Thread plastic darning needles with yarn and knot the ends of the yarn. Let each child make his own design. Some may need help initially with the mechanics of sewing.

CHALK PAINTING
Provide pans of liquid starch mixed with a small amount of water, some large flat paint brushes, smooth paper, and large 1 × 4 inch colored chalk. Let children paint their paper with starch and then make designs on the wet paper with the colored chalk. When product dries, the starch acts as a fixative and chalk does not rub off the paper.

BUTTERMILK CHALK
Dampen table to hold finger-paint paper in place. Place a teaspoonful of buttermilk on paper and let child use chalk through the milk. The buttermilk acts as a carrier and the product is sim-

HELPFUL HINTS

> *Help strengthen small muscles by doing the following:*
> 1. *Provide individual hand paper punches and show children how to hold paper with one hand and squeeze the punch to make holes.*
> 2. *Make "train tickets" for the conductor to punch.*
> 3. *Provide kitchen tongs for children to pick up articles of varying weights, from cotton balls to nuts and bolts.*
> 4. *Space containers at varying distances from each other and ask child to transfer items from one container to the other.*
> 5. *Sew snaps on separate pieces of material and have children snap them together, first by pushing the snaps together against a table top with just the thumb, then first finger, etc.; do the same with the opposite hand. Then have the child hold up the pieces of cloth and snap the snaps together with the thumb and first finger of the right hand, the thumb and last finger of the left hand, and other such variations.*

ilar to finger paint but more easily controlled by child. Also, try using dampened paper towels. Be sure to wash chalk after each use or rub chalk on wire mesh screen to clear off dried starch.

GLASS WAX FUN

Need your windows washed? Rub glass wax all over the window and allow to dry. Let the children draw with their fingers. When they are finished, wipe with clean cloth.

CORN MEAL SANDBOX

Provide children with a partially filled box of corn meal and measuring cups, spoons, sieves. Let the children work on an old shower curtain or tablecloth.

FISHING POLE

Tie a piece of string to a length of doweling or a stick. On the other end of the string, tie a magnet. Let the child fish for bobby pins, clips, etc., in a tub or an old tire which has been cut in half and filled with water.

YARN WEAVING

Dip ends of yarn in melted wax and let children weave in and out of plastic berry baskets.

NAIL BOARD

Hammer small furniture tacks or nails into a rectangular board, about 6" × 8". Give the children a good supply of colored wires, yarns, and rubber bands to stretch across the nails.

SPACKLE PRINTS

Purchase spackling powder at any paint or hardware store. Mix with sufficient water to consistency of whipped cream. Be sure mixture is free of lumps. Pour into cottage cheese carton tops and let children make hand prints. Or add colored powder paint if desired and pour into egg carton lids and let children use collage materials such as jewels, broken bits of crayons, bits of twigs, leaves and natural materials to make design in the spackle. Or pour spackle onto waxed paper and let children use collage materials. Lift off waxed paper when dry. Spackle is far superior to plaster of paris, because it dries more slowly allowing children time to make their imprints and/or change their minds in making designs. The finished product takes 40 minutes to an hour to dry.

SAND CASTING — *Use shells to make imprints in wet sand. Pour in plaster of paris. Remove when hardened. This is also a good way to make candles. Use juice cans, plastic bottles, or other objects to make a deep imprint in wet sand. Insert wick and pour in melted candle wax. Remove when cool and hard.*

STYROFOAM ART — *Save styrofoam meat trays and use them for collage with glue, spackle, or plaster of paris. Use various shapes of macaroni dyed with food coloring to make an impressive display; or collect bits of natural materials such as leaves, rocks, shells, and use as in spackle prints.*

SOAP SNOW — *Whip 2 cups soap flakes with ½ cup water to consistency of thick whipped cream. Use for "frosting" cardboard by pressing through the cooky press or pastry tubes. Dip hand in water before molding with this mixture. Soap snow will dry to a porous texture and last for weeks.*

HELPFUL HINTS

Tie Dyeing

Materials

Untreated soft cotton cloth
String or rubber bands
Powdered or liquid dye (keep adding dye until desired shade is achieved)
Container of clear water
Salt
Container for dye bath, preferably stainless steel or enamel

Procedure

1. Have the dye bath simmering during the entire dyeing process. (For fastness a few tablespoons of salt can be added.)
2. Tie cloth tightly by bunching it up in a ball and tying with string; or pleating it like a fan (stripes); or picking it up in the center and wrapping string around down to the open edge (circle); or experimenting any way you choose.[1] Teacher may need to tighten string or rubber bands after the child has tried.
3. Place tied cloth in the clear water until completely soaked.
4. Remove from water and place in the dye. Let simmer in dye for 1 to 3 minutes, depending on strength of dye and desired shade.
5. Remove from dye (strainer or basket comes in handy) and rinse under faucet until water runs clear.
6. Remove string and repeat the same procedure, omitting dipping in clear water if you want to add another color.

Onion Skin Dyeing

Materials

Bag of onion skins (available free at produce markets)
Eggs
8-inch squares of cloth
Bits of rice, leaves, small flowers
String
Pot for boiling eggs

---

[1] Many beautiful designs are created by accident and most techniques are acquired through practice, experience, and experimentation.

An Activities Handbook for Teachers of Young Children

Procedure

1. Place about 6 to 8 layers of onion skin on each piece of cloth.
2. Place bits of design material, (rice, leaves, or flower petals, etc.) on top of the onion skin.
3. Place an egg on top of the above materials and wrap carefully.
4. Tie the cloth tightly around the egg and onion skin.
5. Put wrapped egg in a pot of water and boil for 30 minutes.
6. Cool and untie egg.

Supplementary learning

1. Explain that this is the way Latvian children used to color their Easter eggs. Onion skin can also be used in tie dyeing by boiling the material and skins together. The color will vary from yellow to brown with the darker shade resulting from longer boiling in a larger quantity of onion skins.
2. Discuss how people of different cultures dye their clothing and materials made from plants, such as how Indian rugs are made. Or use the story of "Pelle's New Suit" to discuss the process of making wool, dyeing it, and finally sewing it into clothing. Children can save shaggy dog hair, wash it and dye it, and use it for collages. For more information on natural dyes, see "Dye Plants and Dyeing—A Handbook," available through the Brooklyn Botanic Garden, Brooklyn, New York.

Footprints

Materials Paint
Large juice cans
Paint brushes
Newsprint
Dishpan of warm, soapy water
Towels
Two small chairs
Large sheet of plastic or oil cloth

Procedure
1. Spread sheet of plastic on floor.
2. Place a long sheet of newsprint on top of plastic.
3. Place a chair at each end of the newsprint.
4. At one end place cans of paint and brushes.
5. At the other end place pan of soapy water and towels.
6. Have children remove their shoes and socks.
7. Have child sit on chair and paint the bottom of his feet with a color he selects.
8. Instruct the child to walk on the paper, leaving his footprints.
9. At the end of the paper, have him step into pan of soapy water to clean his feet.
10. Proceed in the same manner with other children, using the same piece of paper for everyone.

Suggestions
1. Label one of his prints with the child's name, so that he can identify his own footprint.
2. Hang finished product on wall and caption, e.g., "Let's Go Walking."
3. Make a similar mural using hand prints.

Bibliography of Resources

Books About Art Activities*

Carmichael, Viola S. *Curriculum ideas for young children.* Los Angeles: Southern California Association for the Education of Young Children, 1971. This booklet presents ideas for art and craft activities under such topics as homes and families, occupations, community helpers, transportation, and seasons.

Christensen, Fred B. *Recipes for creative art, set 1 basic.* Monterey Park, Ca.: Creative Teaching Press, 1967. A folder full of recipes, each on a separate card. These are primarily for elementary age children but many can be adapted for use at the preschool level. Some of the recipes are for activities such as crayon "batik," glue printing, and some of the basic sponge painting, string painting, mobiles, etc.

---

* See also pages 53–54 for books about colors and shapes.

Connelly, Luella. *Recipes for creative art holidays and seasons, set 2.* Monterey Park, Ca.: Creative Teaching Press, 1968. This folder is designed in the same format as Set 1 described above. These are arranged for reference according to holidays and seasons. For example, there are recipes for dyed eggshell mosaics and colored tissue twirls for spring and stained glass effects with crayon scraps ironed between wax paper. The teacher can use these for ideas to present materials for children to create their own art in their own way.

Croft, Doreen. *Recipes for busy little hands.* Palo Alto, Ca.: 741 Maplewood Pl., 1973. A popular little booklet compiled for use with student teachers in a college nursery school training program. The basic recipes for easel paints, finger paints, graphic and plastic art materials were contributed by teachers from other preschool programs, including an unusual dough recipe from the People's Republic of China. The illustrated booklet also has a section of most-used finger plays and another section of cooking recipes.

Gregg, Elizabeth. *What to do when there's nothing to do.* New York: Delacorte Press, 1968. This is designed as a mother's handbook by members of the staff of the Boston Children's Medical Center. It includes 601 play ideas for young children with good suggestions and information about the interests of preschoolers at the different age levels. The authors provide ideas using simple materials found in the home, such as surprise and comfort bags filled with things like gummed labels and paper, dry cereal, miniature toys, etc., to give to the child when mother has to take him to the doctor or on a trip when he is likely to be bored. Other items call for the use of milk cartons, pots and pans, cereal boxes, old nylons, etc.

Hartley, Ruth E., and Robert M. Goldenson. *The complete book of children's play.* New York: Thomas Y. Crowell, 1963. The chapters deal with children from the first year to their pre-teens. The discussions are centered around interests of children and how the teacher can provide activities which meet their needs at particular levels of development.

Haupt, Dorothy, and Keith D. Osborn. *Creative activities.* Detroit, Mich.: The Merrill Palmer School, 1955. A handbook of activities for the teacher of young children, including such topics as paints, paper activities, nature study, cooking, and woodwork.

Hollander, H. Cornelia. *Portable workshop for pre-school teachers.* New York: Doubleday. This packet consists of ten guides, each a separate booklet designed for the teacher of young children. Booklets cover music and rhythm, painting and gadget prints, scribbling and finger-painting, toys and games.

Hoover, F. Louis. *Art activities for the very young.* Worcester, Mass.: Davis Publications, 1961. The activities presented are for the 3–6 age group covering such things as stitchery, puppets, finger painting, and stenciling. Some of the activities may be too difficult for the very young, but the teacher will find helpful hints and suggestions on involving young children in art activities.

Johnson, June. *Home play for the pre-school child.* New York: Harper & Brothers, 1957. A book of creative crafts and activities with ideas and recipes for different kinds of painting, play dough and clay, making toys, and indoor and outdoor activities. There is also a section on family activities and setting up a play group in the home.

Kauffman, Carolyn, and Patricia Farrell. *If you live with little children.* New York: G. P. Putnam's Sons, 1957. This is a helpful book for parents with small children. There are ideas and drawings for outdoor equipment such as a jungle gym and a rubber tire cut in half for floating boats and many other practical kinds of toys and equipment made from inexpensive materials. The section on indoor play has activities using many inexpensive common objects such as egg cartons, buttons, coffee cans, etc. There are many ideas to help the parent cope with ordinary routines of the day. The teacher may find this a helpful resource book in the school.

Keppler, Hazel. *The child and his play.* New York: Funk & Wagnalls, 1952. The book deals with topics such as choosing toys for preschoolers and the kinds of toys which help to contribute to creative development. Another chapter discusses books and how to select and tell a story. Other topics include art, cooking, developing social understanding, rhythm activities, and evaluating a child's abilities through his play.

McDonald, Pauline, and Doris V. Brown. *Creative art for home and school.* Los Angeles: Du-Mor, 1961. Activities are designed and presented in a format which includes materials, preparation, and procedure. Areas covered include drawing, collage, modeling, holiday projects.

Mergeler, Karen. *Too good to eat! the art of dough sculpture.* Santa Ana, Ca.: Folk Art Publications, 1972. The author traces the history of dough art in ancient cultures with lovely examples and illustrations. She then provides recipes to help the reader explore the magic of the baking art. Includes baker's clay, bread dough, making sculptures, antiquing, and glazing dough. Interesting for the teacher and adaptable to simpler projects for children.

NAEYC Publications. *Water, sand and mud as play materials.* Washington, D.C., 1959. An excellent little booklet providing the teacher with a rationale for the use of plastic and fluid materials in a curriculum for young children. Many ideas for promoting outdoor play with water, sand, mud, clay, etc.

Pitcher, Evelyn Goodenough, *et al. Helping young children learn.* Columbus, Ohio: Charles E. Merrill, 1966. This book is designed for teachers of young children presenting activities and guidelines for the preschool curriculum. Some of the areas include science, art, music, literature, and academic preliminaries with helpful discussions on the role of the teacher.

Books About Art for the Teacher

Bannon, Laura. *Mind your child's art.* New York: Pellegrini & Cudahy, 1952. Useful suggestions to parents and teachers on how to conduct themselves in relation to children's art. Well illustrated with specific pointers on what not to say or do as well as helpful information about how children develop artistically.

Cole, Natalie Robinson. *Children's arts from deep down inside.* New York: John Day, 1966. A beautifully illustrated book with materials and actual verbal interactions gathered from the classroom. The author shows the teacher without any special background in art how she can get creative expression from her children. Art can be an instrument for learning about many things and expressing inner feelings. Designed for primary grades, but should be illuminating for the preschool teacher.

D'Amico, Victor. *Experiments in creative art teaching.* New York:

Doubleday, 1960. A progress report of the Museum of Modern Art with many helpful sections for the teacher of young children, including such topics, as "Questions Often Asked by Parents," "Basic Aims," "Philosophy and Methods;" also included are suggestions for teaching adults.

Eisner, Elliott W., and David W. Ecker (eds.). *Readings in art education*. Waltham, Mass.: Blaisdell, 1966. A variety of views based on research giving the teacher a broad perspective of art education. Some particularly useful articles include "Easel Painting as an Index of Personality in Pre-school Children" by Rose H. Alschuler and Laberta A. Hattwick; "The Psychological Interpretation of Children's Drawings" by Florence L. Goodenough; and "The Child as Painter" by Victor D'Amico.

Greenberg, Pearl (Chm.) *Art education: elementary*. Washington, D.C.: The National Art Education Association, 1972. This compilation of articles was written by a task force of specialists in elementary education. It covers such topics as the child-centered art program, perceptual and behavioral approaches to art, the role of the teacher, and the uses of TV and films.

Hartley, Ruth E., *et al*. *Understanding children's play*. New York: Columbia University Press, 1952. A text based on many observations in the nursery school and case histories conducted by psychologists exploring the value of play experiences for different types of children. The book covers such topics as dramatic play, music and movement, water play as well as the art areas such as clay and painting.

Jameson, Kenneth. *Art and the young child*. New York: Viking, 1968. Art can be a direct source of education for young children. The author emphasizes this viewpoint with many examples of how children paint and draw and how a close study of children's art can help the teacher and parent gain insight into his personality and social background. Includes an excellent section with a special message for the teacher and the parent and the role each should play.

Kellogg, Rhoda. *Analyzing children's art*. Palo Alto, Ca.: National Press Books, 1969. The author has collected half a million children's drawings and paintings since she began teaching nursery school in 1928. Her book traces the development in art form of the two-to-eight age group and classifies the similarities in spontaneous art among children throughout the world.

————, and Scott O'Dell. *The psychology of children's art*. Del Mar, Ca.: CRM-Random House, 1967. Beautiful color illustrations of children's art depicting basic scribbles, designs, and art forms common to all art throughout the world. Scott O'Dell's text helps the reader become aware of the beauty of the "un-adult-erated vision of the child."

Lark-Horovitz, Hilda Present Lewis, and Mark Luca. *Understanding children's art for better teaching*. Columbus, Ohio: Charles E. Merrill, 1967. The authors identify common characteristics of art at each age level. One portion of the book is devoted to the retarded, blind, and handicapped child. A bibliography gives sources of teaching materials including films and slides.

Lewis, Hilda Present (ed.). *Child art, the beginnings of self-affirmation*. Berkeley: Diablo Press, 1966. This publication is a compilation of reports and discussions presented at a conference held at the University of California, Berkeley, on child art. The contributors are among the world's outstanding art educators. Some of the topics include

"The Child's Language of Art," by Arno Stern; "Creativity in Children," by Frank X. Barron; "Questions and Answers About Teaching Art," by Victor D'Amico.

Lindstrom, Miriam. *Children's art, a study of normal development in children's modes of visualization.* Berkeley: University of California Press, 1964. Explores the normal development of visualization between ages 2–15. Discusses children's art at different levels of the developmental process and helps adults understand what art means to the child.

Lowenfeld, Viktor. *Your child and his art, a guide for parents.* New York: Macmillan, 1954. A worthwhile and sensible discussion of child art written by a leading authority in the field for parents and teachers so that they may better understand the work of the child.

Luca, Mark, and Robert Kent. *Art education: strategies of teaching.* Englewood Cliffs, N.J.: Prentice-Hall, 1968. This is a book which discusses child growth and art in the curriculum based on the idea that most art programs in schools stifle the needs of the growing child. Written for elementary school teachers, but some helpful suggestions on such areas as crafts, finger painting, holidays, and marionettes.

Mendelowitz, Daniel M. *Children are artists.* Stanford, Ca.: Stanford University Press, 1953. The text helps parents and teachers understand child art from the scribbler to the adolescent.

Raboff, Ernest. *Art for children.* New York: Doubleday. Each book in this series is a short biographical sketch, with excellent color reproductions, of a famous artist. The descriptions and simple discussion of subject matter provide the teacher and young children with an excellent resource for a better understanding and appreciation of great art. Some of the titles cover Paul Klee, Rembrandt, Toulouse-Lautrec, Dürer.

Tomlinson, R. R. *Children as artists.* London: Penguin, 1947. One of the earlier books written proposing that child art is as appealing to the emotions as adult art. The author describes some of the artistic training of children of the past and speculates on future developments.

Young, Ethel. *The nursery school program for culturally different children.* Menlo Park, Ca.: Pacific Coast Publishers, 1965. This is a notebook which grew out of a need to fill the demand for proven material in designing curricula for compensatory preschool programs. The booklet describes some of the unique learning problems of the socially disadvantaged child and includes programs for art, music and dance activities, and language development.

Music Activities

Rhythm

#1

PURPOSE — *Exploring body response in feeling rhythm*

Materials — For teacher use: piano or recorded instrumental music and record player

HELPFUL HINTS

> *Select a book such as* Waltzing Matilda, *by A. B. Paterson (New York: Holt, Rinehart & Winston, 1970), and explore the rhythm of words like "coolabah," "billabong," and "tucker-bag" from this well-known Australian song.*

Procedure

1. Have children find a place to sit where they can put their hands out and not touch anyone. Play a selection which has the ABA form (starts with Theme A, changes to Theme B, and ends with Theme A again). For example, start with a simple melody like "Baa baa, black sheep, have you any wool? Yes sir, yes sir, three bags full" (Theme A). "One for my master and one for my dame, and one for the little boy who lives in the lane" (Theme B). Then repeat Theme A.
2. Ask them to listen to the song once. Sing or play any bouncy song which is popular with them.[2]
3. Say (while playing music):
Now as I play the music I want you to move your body the way the music makes you feel.
4. The next time you play say:
This time do something different.
5. When you stop playing note some of the changes children made.
6. Encourage them to stand up and move as you play.

Variation

Use drum to beat a rhythm.

Rhythm

#2

PURPOSE

Exploring body as rhythm instrument

Materials

For teacher use: piano or recorded instrumental music[3] and record player

Procedure

1. Have children sit on floor.
2. Ask:
Who can make a sound using his or her hands? (Possibilities include clapping, slapping various parts of the body, snapping fingers, clapping with cupped hands, etc.)
If you stand up what new sounds can you make? (Possibilities

---

[2] Other suggestions: "Raindrops Are Falling" from the score of "Butch Cassidy and the Sundance Kid" (A&M Records SP4227); "Pop Goes The Weasel" (RCA Victor 45-6180); "The Tartan Ball" (EMI SZLP2118).

[3] Suggestion: "Taos Round Dance" (Canyon ARP142)—a subdued Indian record good for quiet movements as well as rocking, shaking, sliding, shuffling.

include stamping, shuffling, tapping toes, sliding feet, heel-toe action.)

What are some of the sounds you can make with your mouth? (Possibilities include tongue clacking, teeth clicking, lip smacking, hissing and sighing, etc.)

3. Play different kinds of music and let them respond in any way they wish.

Rhythm

#3

PURPOSE   *Hearing rhythm in words*

Materials   None

Procedure   1. Sit with children in a circle.
                 2. Say:
                 Remember how you clapped time to the music?
                 Do you know that your names have a rhythm?
                 I am going to say the names of some of you.
                 3. Go around the circle saying the names of the children with one-syllable names, e.g., John, Ruth, Ann. Then say a two-syllable name, e.g., Mary, Richard, Warren. Ask whether they hear anything different about the two-syllable names.
                 4. Ask them to clap when you say "John" or whatever (clap). Then ask them to clap when you say "Richard" (clap, clap).
                 5. Say the three-syllable names. Ask the children to clap.

> *A good book to use for exploring rhythm, chanting, singing, and language development is* Mandala, *by Arnold Adoff (New York: Harper & Row, 1971). From the Sanskrit word* mandala, *which means "magic circle," the author develops a poem chanted by an African family.*

6. Either in this session or in a future one organize the children into a group according to the syllables in their name. Have them clap the appropriate pattern according to their names. Ask them how the three groups could work together with their claps to make interesting rhythm. They could try clapping at the same time and hear how three beats take longer than one or two, if rhythm is the same. They could alternate rhythmic patterns.

Variation Read nonsense rhymes or poems and have children clap to the rhythm of the words they like.

Rhythm

#4

PURPOSE *Learning to play rhythm instruments*

Materials Drums and mallets (heads can be covered with lambswool) tambourines, coconut half-shells, wood blocks, finger cymbals, triangles, sand blocks, rhythm sticks, sleigh bells on leather bracelets, and maracas (if choice is limited, using drums, triangles and sand blocks provide good contrasts)

Procedure
1. Use music with which the children are familiar and which has a lively rhythmic pattern.
2. Put the instruments out and allow the children to experiment. If there is one drum per child, drums should be used first.
3. Ask individual children as they play whether they could play another way. Encourage them to hit the drum on various parts of the head and to use different rhythmic patterns.
4. Play loud music, then soft music; slow music, then fast music.
5. The children could play a "call and response" game either in groups or by taking turns being the originator.
6. Use this same procedure to introduce the other rhythm instruments.

Rhythm

#5

PURPOSE *Reproducing rhythmic sounds*

Materials	Empty cardboard cartons, such as those used for oatmeal
Procedure	1. Make up a story based on the children's everyday experiences at home and in school.
	2. Tell the story, using the empty carton to produce appropriate sound effects. For example:
	Early in the morning, before it was time to get up for school, Johnny heard shuffle, shuffle (rub hand across top of carton to make a rhythmic shuffling sound).
	What was that? It was mother shuffling to the kitchen in her slippers. Johnny closed his eyes and listened again. Then he heard . . . , etc.
	3. Use simple rhythmic sounds at first, such as click, click, click (scrambling eggs with a fork); clump, clump (Dad's footsteps); tap, tap, tap, tap (the dog). Then increase in difficulty with combinations of sounds—bump, bump, bumpety, bump (brother going down the stairs, dog dragging a slipper or playing with a ball, etc.)
	4. After the children have had several opportunities to listen and watch how the teacher does it, select two or three children to help tell a story.
	5. Give each of the selected children a carton. Vary the story so they have to listen and watch.
	6. Over a period of time, gradually increase the size of the group of storytellers and vary the rhythmic sounds as the children become more skilled. Have them guess occasionally about what the sound represents.
	7. Start simply and proceed slowly. The purpose of the activity is to give children practice in listening and reproducing sounds. Keep the story short at first. Handing out too many cartons can cause distraction and confusion. Limit the number until children understand the purpose for which they are intended.

Rhythm

#6

Purpose	*Identifying rhythmic sounds*
Materials	Tape recorder
Procedure	1. Identify and tape rhythmic sounds familiar to the children, such as walking, dancing, hammering, sawing, snoring, bouncing a ball, hopping, typing, clapping hands, chewing, clicking the tongue, breathing, using an egg beater, brushing teeth, etc.
	2. Play each one and have children guess what the sounds are. Allow plenty of time for guessing, questioning, and discussing. Give clues to help, and encourage children to try to reproduce the human sounds.
	3. Have children help decide what kinds of rhythmic sounds the class should tape for other guessing games.

HELPFUL HINTS

1. *Invite local musicians, perhaps high-school students, to perform.*
2. *Children will often laugh at the sounds of instruments unfamiliar to them.*
3. *Prepare performers from the community by helping them understand that young children are curious, have a short attention span, want to touch and talk about and try out instruments for themselves. Try to plan a presentation that is short and will allow children to satisfy their natural curiosity.*

4. Let the children who can identify the sounds be the "teacher" and ask questions and give clues to the others.

Tone

#1

PURPOSE   *Recognizing high and low sounds*

Materials   For teacher use: piano or other musical instrument

Procedure
1. Have the children sit on the floor and listen while you play first a middle C and follow it with a C an octave higher. Repeat this twice.
2. Ask:
   Did both of those notes sound the same?
   What can you do to show me when you hear the high note?
   What can you do for the low note?
3. Play the notes again and let them respond in the agreed upon manner.
4. Use another instrument such as resonator bells, resonator blocks, harmonica, or any bells or whistle.
5. Play a melody on the piano or record player which has obvious high and low changes in it, and have the children respond by stretching high for the high notes and crouching low for the low notes.

Tone

#2

PURPOSE   *Experiencing loud and soft*

Materials   For the children and the teacher: one paper megaphone each

Procedure
1. Ask the children to make their voices loud when your voice is loud, soft when your voice is soft.
2. Sing a call-response song.
3. Vary the pattern of loud-soft, do not just alternate the two. If you build up to three or four soft versions before you do a loud

one, you will create a sense of anticipation in the children. Stop and ask them what they felt like while waiting for the loud sound. Explain that composers do the same thing.

4. Play examples from a variety of recordings to demonstrate.[4]

[4] Suggestions: Bowmar Orchestral Library—Bowmar Records: "Classroom Concert" (Bol. 68); "Miniatures in Music" (Bol 64); "Fairy Tales in Music" (Bol 57); "Adventures in Music—Grade 1" (RCA Victor LE-1000); "Concert in the Park" (RCA Victor LM-2677); "The Light Music of Shostakovich" (Columbia LM-6267); "Gaiete Parisienne"—Offenbach (Columbia ML-5348).

HELPFUL HINTS

> 1. Tape the children singing some of their favorite songs and play them back.
> 2. Play music in the art area and let children paint to music.
> 3. Turn the lights off or down low and listen to a music box.
> 4. Play restful music during snack time.
> 5. Use a special record as a signal for transition from one activity to another.

Tone

#3

PURPOSE
Learning that different instruments have different sounds

Materials
Records with a variety of instrumental solos
Pictures of people playing those instruments

Procedure
1. Show a picture of someone playing a violin.
2. Play a record with a violin solo, play another solo which is a different style (e.g., first a classical piece, then "Hot Canary" or "Pop Goes the Weasel").
3. Then play a trumpet solo for contrast. Show a picture of the trumpet.
4. Show the children how to pretend they are playing a violin.
5. If possible find a violinist to come and play for the children.
6. Use this same procedure to introduce a woodwind (clarinet, flute), a brass instrument (trumpet), and a percussion instrument.

Melody

#1

PURPOSE
Learning to sing a song from memory

Materials
For teacher use: guitar or piano or autoharp (optional)

Procedure
1. Choose a simple song which is repetitious.
2. Sing it casually during free play so that the children become familiar with it.
3. Introduce it during formal music time, play it at least once and then ask whether anyone wants to help sing.
4. Ask for requests. If the children choose they will have more incentive to sing along.

Melody

#2

PURPOSE
Learning to identify identical melodies

Materials	For teacher use: piano, guitar, or records and record player
Procedure	1. Have the children sit on the floor.
	2. Play one melody, e.g., "Baa, Baa, Black Sheep," several times. Then play another melody, and then play "Baa, Baa, Black Sheep" again.
	3. Ask the children to raise their hands when they hear the first melody again. Then play another new melody. Then play "Baa, Baa, Black Sheep" once again, asking them to raise their hands when the melody is familiar.
	4. Go through the sequence again using two or three more non-matching melodic phrases between the familiar melody.
	5. This game can be made more challenging for older children by using songs with similar melodic directions and rhythmic patterns.

Melody

#3

PURPOSE	*Learning to play a melodic instrument, creating original melodies*
Materials	For children's use: piano, resonator blocks, resonator bells, or a xylophone
Procedure	1. If using a piano or xylophone, one child can use the instrument at a given time. If using the bells or resonator blocks, children can use the instruments to create three sequential tones at first, building up to four, five, six, and more.
	2. Encourage the children to experiment with the sound sequences.
	3. Ask if they can play the same melody twice.
	4. As children become more knowledgeable, they can play a game of matching each other's melodies.

Text

PURPOSE	*Learning to listen to and respond to words in a song*
Materials	For teacher use: piano, guitar, autoharp, or records and record player
Procedure	1. Ask the children to listen very carefully and do what they feel like doing. (You can play songs about animals which the children could imitate, or work songs, or instructive songs ["Put Your Finger in the Air"], or songs that tell a story.)
	2. Play at least three different kinds so the children can talk about how songs are used for many different purposes.[5]

---

[5] The Children's Music Center, 5373 W. Pico Blvd., Los Angeles, Ca., 90019, has a catalog which categorizes records according to purpose, such as music for "resting time," "language development," "community," etc.

Mood

#1

PURPOSE   *Responding to the mood of a song*

Materials For teacher use: piano, guitar, autoharp, or records and record player

Procedure 1. Ask the children to listen carefully to the song and move to the music if they want to do so.
2. Play a series of songs each with a different mood—happy, sad, scary, peaceful.[6]
3. After each song or instrumental, ask the children how the music made them feel. What did it make them think of? Do they know another song which makes them feel the same?

Mood

#2

PURPOSE   *Learning how the composer uses the music to complement the text*

Materials For teacher use: record ("Peter and the Wolf" [Leonard Bernstein and N.Y. Philharmonic on Columbia] and record player)

Procedure 1. Play the record in one session simply as a listening experience to familiarize the children with the story.
2. During the second session, listen several times to the first part, which associates themes with animals. Talk about how the sounds describe the animals.
3. Have the children take turns acting out the story with each child assigned a theme.

Form

#1

PURPOSE   *Learning that music has a form—a beginning, a middle, and an end*

Materials For teacher use: a piano, guitar, autoharp, or record and record player

Procedure 1. Ask children to stand, spacing themselves out.

---

[6] Suggestions: "Suites from Gayne" (Khatchaturian, Capitol P8503); "The Courtly Dances from Gloriana" (Britten, Victor LM 2730); "Zorba, the Greek" (20th Century Fox TFM3167); "Going Places" (Herb Alpert's Tijuana Brass, A&M Records LP112); "Souvenirs From Sweden (Epic LF18010); "Toshiba Singing Angels" (Capitol T10252); "The Beatles' Yellow Submarine" (Capitol Records SW153).

1. Knowing how to play a musical instrument can be a real asset in applying for a job with young children.

2. Call your local music store and inquire about guitar rentals and lessons.

3. If you learn just two simple chords on the guitar (A, E7), you will be able to play all these songs and more: "This Old Man," "My Dreydl," "Hush Little Baby," "Old MacDonald Had a Farm," "Row, Row, Row Your Boat," "Polly Wolly Doodle," "Clementine," "Go Tell Aunt Rhody," "Billy Boy," "On Top of Old Smoky," "Old Susanna."

A

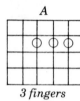

3 fingers

E7

2 fingers

2. Tell them you are going to play parts of a song and they are to move to the music and stop as soon as the music stops.
3. Play short phrases of a lively tune.[7] Gradually play several phrases together. Then play the whole piece.
4. Contrast the lively piece by playing a slow, flowing song.[8] Have the children lie on the floor and move their arms to the music.

Variations

1. Set up chairs in a circle, one per child. Ask the children to begin moving around the chairs when the music starts and sit down on a chair as soon as it stops.
2. Give the children rhythm instruments to play with the music.

Form

#2

PURPOSE

Learning that music has patterned forms

Materials

For teacher use: a piano, guitar, autoharp, or record and record player

For children's use: set of triangles for half of the children; set of drums for the other half of the children

Procedure

1. Play a selection which has the ABA form (starts with theme A, changes to theme B, and ends with theme A again).
2. Give half the children triangles (or appropriate substitute).

---

[7] Bouncy, lively records: "The Tartan Ball" (EMI SZLP2118); "Pop Goes the Weasel" (RCA Victor 45–6180).

[8] Slow, flowing records: "Duets With Spanish Guitar" (Capitol 8406); "Songs in Spanish for Children" (Columbia 91A02029).

Play the first theme again. Then tell them that is the "A" theme; that is their part. When they hear that theme they can play along on their triangles.

3. Give the drums to the other half of the class. Play the "B" theme, identify it as such and tell the children with drums that is their theme. Ask what they will do when they hear their theme.

4. Ask children to listen while you play the whole "ABA" pattern again.

5. Ask them to play their instruments when they hear their themes this time.

6. After the children have done this exercise several times, encourage them to find new combinations as they play without music, i.e.: AABB, ABBA.

Bibliography of Resources

Activity Song Books

Crowninshield, Ethel. *Stories that sing.* Boston: Boston Music Company, 1955. Each page of the book is a short story with portions of the story set to music. For example, a story about "Lucky Lucy" tells how Lucy got lost, but how she was lucky because she remembered her address. The story ends with children singing "Lucky little Lucy, lucky as can be! Lucy lived on Lucky Street, number twenty-three." Music and words are illustrated with pictures created by kindergarten children.

Groetzinger, Isabelle, and Marguerite Gode. *Play and sing, Hayes action song book for kindergarten and primary.* Wilkinsburg, Pennsylvania: Hayes School Publishing Co., 1958. Action songs with words and piano music. Each song is accompanied by an illustration and suggestions for the teacher to involve the children in making appropriate movements to go along with the song. Some of the action songs include "My Pony" (Children gallop at a fast and slow pace), "Let's Play Store," "Windmill Song," and other songs for special holidays.

Miller, Mary, and Paula Zajan. *Finger play.* New York: G. Schirmer, 1955. A collection of simple, illustrated finger plays with accompanying piano music. The "Songs for Little Fingers" include "Ten Little Indians," "Join in the Game," "Where is Thumpkin?" and "I'm a Little Teapot."

Norman, Ruth. *Action songs for special occasions.* New York: Mills Music Co. A series of action songs for special occasions such as Washington's birthday, Valentine's Day, Halloween, etc., in sheet music form. Each set of songs includes suggestions for dramatization through hand movements and body rhythms.

Richards, Mary Helen. *Mary Helen Richards teaches: the child in depth.* Portola Valley, Ca.: Richards Institute of Music Education and Research, 1969. This book is designed for the kindergarten and early primary teacher who wants to develop techniques for teaching language arts by involving the whole child in movement exploration.

The author uses simple songs to teach form, rhythm, and tone with emphasis on the systematic development of visual, auditory, and motor coordination of the child. Based on the Kodaly Method, which incorporates music into the total curriculum.

Winn, Marie; Allan Miller; and Karla Kushkin. *What shall we do and allee galloo!* New York: Harper & Row, 1970. Play songs and singing games all set to music. There are finger-play songs, follow-the-leader songs, word play, and simple games such as "This is the Way We Wash Our Hands," "The Little Pony," and "Peek-a-Boo." Attractively illustrated.

Song Books

Association for Childhood Education International and Division of Christian Education National Council of the Churches of Christ in the United States of America. *Songs children like, folk songs from many lands.* Washington, D.C.: Association for Childhood Education International, 1958. A collection of songs with piano accompaniment from the United States and other countries. The songs include well known favorites such as "Hush, Li'l' Baby," "My Dredyl," and some less well known favorites such as the Japanese "Haru Ga Kita," the Latin American "La Muneca," and "Chinese Lullaby."

Bailey, Charity, and Eunice Holsaert. *Sing a song with Charity Bailey.* New York: Plymouth Music Company, 1955. English versions of twenty popular folk songs for children from such countries as Mexico, Haiti, Brazil, Nigeria. The songs have simple piano arrangements and chords for guitar and autoharp. Some include drum rhythms. Also included is Charity Bailey's famous theme song "Hello, Ev'rybody." Others are "Sambalele," "Same Train," "Tum Balalaika."

Chroman, Eleanor. *Songs that children sing.* New York: Oak Publications, 1970. The author has compiled 71 international folk songs for children, some with English translations. Charming photographs of the world's children accompany the guitar chords and piano arrangements.

Dietz, Betty Warner, and Thomas Choonbai Park. *Folk songs of China, Japan, Korea.* New York: John Day, 1964. These simple folk songs are arranged with piano accompaniment; lyrics appear in both English and their original Oriental pronunciations. In addition, the lyrics are written in oriental characters. There are notes on pronunciation, suggestions to the teacher about using the songs to teach customs, history, geography. The lists of records and songbooks are useful for the teacher who wishes to expand the children's music experiences to include the oriental cultures.

Jenkins, Ella; Sherman Krane; and Peggy Lipschutz. *The Ella Jenkins song book for children.* New York: Oak Publications, 1966. The book contains twenty-six songs and chants which the author found she used most in children's groups. They include many songs which encourage children to participate and respond, such as "Hello," and "You'll Sing a Song and I'll Sing a Song." Piano accompaniments and suggestions for leader and group activities.

Landeck, Beatrice. *Echoes of Africa in folk songs of the Americas.* New York: David McKay, 1961. A collection of songs from cultures which have been influenced by African music—Haiti, Creole, Cuba, Puerto Rico, Calypso, Mexico, Panama, etc. There are street cries, work songs, minstrel songs, some familiar and others which had never been written down. Each section has a descriptive text and the piano arrangements include percussion rhythms. The list of records and books should be helpful to the teacher who wants to expose her children to African-influenced music.

————. *Songs to grow on.* New York: Edward B. Marks Music Corporation; William Sloane Associates, 1950. A collection of American folk songs for children including such favorites as "Jennie Jenkins," "Go Tell Aunt Rhody," "The Blue Tail Fly," and "Skip to My Lou." The songs include piano and some rhythm band arrangements. Rhythmic activities and dramatizations are also suggested with some of the songs.

————, and Elizabeth Crook. *Wake up and sing!* New York: Edward B. Marks Music Corporation; William Morrow, 1969. "Folk songs from America's grass roots, selected and adapted for young children with teaching suggestions." The book includes fifty songs and rhymes from such greats as Woody Guthrie and Huddie Ledbetter. The appendices have much helpful information for the teacher, including guitar chords and instructions, a list of record albums, how to tune water glasses, etc. The titles of songs are also grouped to teach such things as awareness of self, family, others, environment, sound, melody, form, etc.

Leodhas, Sorche Nic. *A Scottish songbook.* New York: Holt, Rinehart & Winston, 1969. A collection of sixteen songs which are poems written in the Scottish dialect, illustrated by Evaline Ness. These Scottish airs date from 1530 to 1803. A glossary provides the meanings of unfamiliar words.

McCall, Adeline. *This is music, for kindergarten and nursery school.* Boston: Allyn & Bacon, 1965. Words and music to songs for young children. Sections include "Friends and Family," "Animals," "Singing Through the Day," "Answer-Back Songs," "The Sound of Words," and "Movement."

McLaughlin, Roberta, and Patti Schliestett. *The joy of music, early childhood.* Evanston, Ill.: Summy-Birchard Company, 1967. A collection of songs for young children organized to teach singing, rhythm, various instruments, and other activities. Carefully indexed according to subjects, such as "Air Travel," "Chants," "Folk Music," "Foreign Language Songs," etc., and according to activities such as "Contrasts," "Dramatic Play," and "Quiet Listening," etc.

Nye, Robert; Vernice Nye; Neva Aubin; and George Kyme. *Singing with children.* Belmont, Ca.: Wadsworth, 1962. A collection of songs for the elementary grades, but the teacher of young children will find the sections on action songs and singing games useful. The book also includes a section of songs accompanied by the autoharp and ukelele and songs accompanied by percussion instruments. Teaching objectives are listed at the beginning of each section and the songs include suggestions for other uses.

Reynolds, Malvina. *Little boxes, and other handmade songs.* New York: Oak Publications, 1964. Malvina Reynolds is a delightful protester. She says "This book could be called 'Singin' Mad'. But you can't be meaningfully angry unless you burn because you care truly about people and small children and birds, fishes, ladybugs, and wilderness places, and there are songs here about all that." Her book of songs includes such titles as "Upside Down," "You Can't Make A Turtle Come Out," "Morningtown Ride," and "The Faucets Are Dripping." Guitar chords and melody accompany each song.

Seeger, Ruth Crawford. *American folk songs for children, in home, school, and nursery school.* New York: Doubleday, 1948. The author originally compiled these folk songs for use at a cooperative nursery school. The preface contains a very good discussion on the rationale for introducing young children to American folk music with suggestions for the parent and teacher on improvising, accompanying, and using the songs at home and school. The classified index includes such topics as "Name Play," "Finger Play," "Small Dramas," "Buttons," "Babies," and "Days of the Week."

White, Florence, and Kazuo Akiyama. *Children's songs from Japan.* New York: Edward B. Marks Music Corporation, 1960. This collection of Japanese songs for children is designed in an easy-to-use format. The piano arrangements are simple and the words to the songs are easy-to-pronounce Japanese syllables with accompanying English words. There are singing games, songs about seasons and festivals, street cries, and songs about creatures large and small. Many of the songs have short explanatory introductions with interesting information about Japanese culture.

Winn, Marie (ed.); Allan Miller; and John Alcorn. *The fireside book of children's songs.* New York: Simon & Schuster, 1966. A good collection of songs including sections on Nursery Songs, ("Pop Goes The Weasel," "Eency Weency Spider," "Aiken Drum"), Silly songs ("Bill Grogan's Goat," "There Was A Man And He Was Mad," "Horse Named Bill") and Singing Games and Rounds ("Clap Your Hands," "The Hokey-Pokey," "Kookaburra"). Piano arrangements.

Where to Write for Additional Resource Materials

The following organizations will provide catalogues and lists of records, song books, information about aids for the teacher of music, and musical activities for the young child:

Association for Childhood Education International
3615 Wisconsin Avenue, N.W.
Washington, D.C. 20016

Bank Street College of Education Bookstore
69 Bank Street
New York, New York 10014

Children's Music Center
5373 West Pico Blvd.
Los Angeles, California 90019

Children's Record Guild
27 Thompson Street
New York, New York

Educational Resources Information Center
4936 Fairmont Avenue
Bethesda, Maryland 20014

Folkways/Scholastic Records
906 Sylvan Avenue
Englewood Cliffs, New Jersey 07632

Creative Activities

Creative Expression

#1

PURPOSE *Learning to imagine and project feelings*

Materials Pictures from magazines and other sources mounted on heavy
tagboard
Pictures should depict such situations as:
mother scolding or spanking a child
two children fighting
serious accident
joyous interactions among people

Procedure 1. Hold pictures up one at a time for children to see.
2. Let them volunteer their observations. (Most will be descriptive. Give children plenty of time to talk about the pictures.)
3. Then ask:
What is happening in this picture?
What do you think happened just before this picture?
and later in the discussion:
What do you think will happen next?
How do you think the story will end?
4. Repeat some of the stories from beginning to end in order to help children recognize that a picture can stimulate imaginings of the past and present and future, as well as project their own wishes.

Creative Expression

#2

PURPOSE *Recognizing and expressing feelings*

Materials Pictures from magazines or other sources mounted on heavy tagboard
Pictures should depict individuals in emotional states such as:
man crying
person looking sad
child who is hurt
woman looking exasperated
other dramatic facial expressions (use very old as well as very young faces)

Procedure 1. Hold pictures up one at a time for children to see, or if working with an individual child, let him hold it and examine it closely.
2. Say:
Tell me about this picture. (Many first responses will be

1. *Recreate experiences and have children act them out.*
   Examples: Pantomine picking out a piece of wrapped candy;
   unwrap it, throw the wrapper in waste basket, chew
   and taste the candy.
   Spread mustard, ketchup, relish on a hot dog and
   eat it.
   Pour sugar and cream into coffee or tea; stir it,
   cool it, taste it.
2. *Recreate feelings and have children express them.*
   Examples: Pantomime pouring a glass of milk and spilling it.
   Scoop up some ice cream into a cone and drop it.
   Pick beautiful flowers and smell them.
   Encourage expression of feelings rather than "superficial"
   acting.

simple identification. Let all children have plenty of opportunity to comment.)
Look at this person's face. How do you think he feels?
(Usually the responses will be simple descriptions.)

3. Continue to encourage all the children to look at details of expression. Say:

Look at his eyes. Do your eyes ever get that way? Look at his mouth. Can we try to make our mouths like that? When do you look like that? (Children will volunteer personal and sometimes seemingly unrelated experiences.)

4. The teacher needs to be aware of, respond to, and encourage the children's individual expressions of feeling.

Creative Expression

#3

PURPOSE
Expressing inner feelings through color, line, movement, shape, and form

Materials
Color pictures and photographs depicting scenes such as:
a colorful day in fall or spring
a wintry landscape
a dismal, dreary scene
a bright and cheerful scene
(Try to avoid scenes emphasizing people)

Procedure
1. Hold pictures up one at a time for children to see. Let them comment on what they see.
2. Say:
   Look at the colors! (Children will usually begin to name them.)
   How does this color make you feel?
   How do all the colors in the whole picture make you feel? I wonder why? (Young children will have difficulty expressing their inner responses to color. The purpose is to call their attention to the effects colors can have.)
3. Repeat the same procedure with line. Say:
   Look at how the artist made his brush strokes go (up/down). Are these lines straight or crooked? Notice the thick paint and the big hard lines. Do you think these lines help to make you feel (happy/sad, etc.)?
4. Comment on the movement in the pictures. Ask:
   What is happening to the leaves in this picture?
   What is moving?
   Why is the girl's hair back like that? What makes your hair do that?
6. Comment on the other shapes in the pictures. Ask:
   How do you think this feels—round or flat?
   Let's try to think about how the artist made this look round instead of flat.
7. Comment on the textures within the pictures. Ask:
   Do you think this is rough or smooth?
   I wonder why it looks (rough/smooth). (Do not expect young children to contribute sophisticated comments at first. They should be given many, many opportunities to learn to look at pictures, people, and nature from the standpoint of the characteristics of color, line, form, etc.)

HELPFUL HINTS

> 1. *Display poster reproductions of famous art. These are available in museum shops and art stores.*
> 2. *Purchase color slides from museums or art departments of local schools and project them for children to talk about.*
> 3. *Read about famous modern art—for example, Jackson Pollock's "Blue Poles"—and have children try some of the same techniques.*

Creative Expression[9]

#4

PURPOSE

Learning that art is a medium of expression

Materials

Reproductions of paintings that deal with the same subject
Examples of paintings that all deal with the subject "children" are:
  "A Girl With a Broom"—Rembrandt (Dutch)
  "Portrait of a Boy"—Soutine (Russian)
  "A Girl With a Watering Can"—Renoir (French)
  "Don Emanuel Osorio De Zuniga—Goya (Spanish)
  "Girl With Braids"—Modigliani (Italian)
Other subjects might be "birds and animals," "flowers," "work," "places"

Procedure

1. Begin discussion by saying:
   When we look at children we see that they do not always look the same. If you are sad your face will look a certain way. (Let child demonstrate.)
   If you are feeling very happy your face might look quite different.
   Many things make us see the same children in different ways.
2. Darken the room and have children look at each other.
3. Introduce a light and say:
   Light can come into a room and change the way a child looks.
4. Introduce the paintings by placing them on low tables or on the floor.
5. Have the children look at the paintings and tell you which one they like best and why.
6. It is interesting to keep a list of the number of children who chose each painting.
7. Encourage the children to use easel paints to "tell" about the way they feel.

---

[9] Adapted from "Elementary Level Pilot Program, Art Appreciation: A Step Toward Aesthetic Awareness," pp. 1–7, prepared by the Palo Alto Unified School District.

AN ACTIVITIES HANDBOOK FOR TEACHERS OF YOUNG CHILDREN

8. Discuss how artists also "tell" the way they feel through their paintings.
9. Discuss how color and light affect the way a person feels.

Creative Expression

#5

PURPOSE   *Learning about three-dimensional objects*

Materials   Paper large enough for a mural
Three-dimensional objects such as driftwood, sculptures, fruits, vegetables, rocks, flowers, sea shells, nuts, etc.

Procedure   1. Select several items which have different textures.
2. Talk to the children about how the objects feel.
3. Have the children close their eyes, give them an object and ask if they can tell what it is by touching and feeling it.
4. Have them turn each object over and look at it another way.
5. Take the children on a nature walk to collect three-dimensional objects.

6. Have the children cooperate in making a large wall mural with the objects they collect.
7. Hang the mural low enough so children can touch it.

Creative Expression

#6

PURPOSE   *Creating stories*

Materials   Paper, felt tip pens or typewriter, heavy construction paper or other material suitable for book cover, staples, yarn, paper punch

Procedure   1. Have child dictate a story.
               2. Print or type his story clearly on paper which has been folded into a book shape.
               3. Let child draw pictures in his book to accompany the story.
               4. Read his story to the other children.

Variations   1. Take a picture of a family member or someone familiar to the child. Show him the picture and ask him to dictate a story about the person. Make it into a book to read.
               2. When a child has had a particularly frightening or exciting experience, help him to share it by dictating it for a book.
               3. Read *I Know What I Like,* by Simon, or *Sometimes I Get Angry,* by Watson et al. and discuss feelings. (See descriptions of these and other books dealing with feelings on pages 58–61, Books About Other Childhood Experiences.)

PUPPETS/#1   Use a small paper bag with face drawn on. Make a hole for the mouth so the child can poke his fingers through for a "tongue." Two fingers can be the "ears."

PUPPETS/#2   *Use an old mitten or sock with buttons for eyes and nose. A small piece of colored material can be used for the mouth and yarn for the hair.*

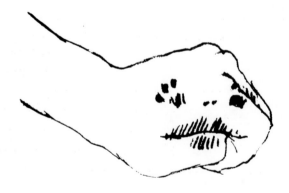

PUPPETS/#3	*A hand can be a puppet. Using a washable marker draw eyes, nose and mouth in the creases of the child's palm. By moving his fingers and stretching them, he can create many amusing expressions.*
PUPPETS/#4	*Use a potato or apple to make a puppet. Cut a hole large enough for the child's finger. With toothpicks, stick on some of the features using slices of olives, cloves, or pieces of the potato or apple. A handkerchief wrapped around the hand becomes a body.*
DRAMATIC PLAY KITS	*The young child recreates and integrates many of his experiences through fantasy and dramatic play. It is in this way that he "makes sense" out of his world. The teacher can help provide many opportunities for dramatic play by supplying the "props" in the school environment and encouraging both boys and girls to assume a variety of roles. Chairs can become trains, cars, boats, or a house. A table covered with a blanket or bedspread becomes a cave or special hiding place. Cardboard cartons which children can decorate convert into houses, forts, or fire stations. Following are some suggested dramatic play kits:*
SUPERMARKET	*Cash register, play money, paper pads, pencils or crayons, punchers, paper sacks, empty food cartons, wax food, grocery boxes, cans with smooth edges.*
BEAUTY PARLOR	*Plastic brushes, combs, make-up, cotton balls, scarves, clip-on rollers, colored water in nail polish bottles, empty hair spray cans, wigs.*
COOKING	*Pots, pans, egg beaters, spoons, pitchers, salt and flour shakers, medicine bottles with colored water, table cloth, aprons.*
POST OFFICE	*Index card file, stamp pads, stampers, crayons, pencils, Christmas stamps, old envelopes.*
SHOE SHINE KIT	*Small cans of clear (natural) polish, sponges, buffers, soft cloth.*
CLEANING SET	*Small brooms, mops, cake of soap, sponges, toweling, plastic spray bottle, plastic basin, clothes line, clothes pins, doll clothes to wash.*
DOCTOR AND NURSE	*Tongue depressers, stethoscope, satchel, adhesive bandages, cotton balls, uniforms, discarded plastic hypo syringes without needles (available from clinics, should be cleaned).*
POSTMAN	*Hats, badges, envelopes, mail satchel.*
FIREMAN	*Hats, raincoats, boots, short length of garden hose.*

FARMER	*Shovel, rake, hoe, seeds.*
PLUMBER	*Wrench, plastic pipes, tool kit.*
GAS STATION ATTENDANT	*Shirt, hat, tire pump.*
HOUSE PAINTER	*Paint brushes, buckets filled with water.*
WINDOW WASHER	*Bucket, soap, sponges, squeegee, water.*
POLICEMAN	*Hat, badge.*
MILKMAN	*Plastic bottles and cartons, wagon, white hat and coat.*

Creative Movement

Guidelines and Procedure

Some types of dancing involve following a pattern of movements the dancer has already been taught. These movements are "right" and "wrong" according to the judgment of the teacher, the goal being a performance for others of a practiced and perfected skill. However, creative movement is not such a performing art. It is, rather, a non-intellectual activity, in which the dancer forgets about himself and allows the music to carry the body away from careful, conscious thinking. Dancing for the child under this philosophy becomes a successful experience filled with music, freedom, and joy. The feeling of success is engendered by the positive and approving attitude of the teacher. Therefore, the role of the teacher in guiding creative movement is of primary importance. The following are basic concepts which the teacher will need to know when she works with young children in this area:

1. The teacher should make it clear that anything the child does will be all right.
2. The child should realize that he needn't do anything that anyone else does; he can do anything the music "tells" him to do.
3. The dance is an integrating experience, pulling the separate parts together, and strengthening and uniting the whole person.
4. Creative dance hopefully provides rewarding interaction between muscular, emotional, and intellectual growth.
5. The teacher can explain that it is all right if the child wants to "copy" someone for a start as they could never look exactly alike.

6. The teacher should make it very clear that each child is different and we all move in a different way.

7. She can explain that dancing is a healthy form of exercise for everyone, and that it takes no special talent or skill.

8. Children should be helped to experience the feeling of freedom in movement, of relationship of movement to space, of relationship to others.

The following is an example of the procedure to follow:

1. Have available a variety of types of musical recordings and a simple long-playing phonograph. Pre-marking bands helps to find appropriate music more readily.

2. Suggest that all the children stand in a circle, facing in.

3. Play a bouncy kind of record, e.g., songs by the Tijuana Brass, and tell the children to feel the bouncing from their tummies and to begin by lightly jumping up and down.[10]

4. The stomach area is the center of the whole body and after bouncing it the children can start bouncing other parts of the body—hands, head, legs, ears, nose—so that everything is more loose than it was.

5. Tell them they can go anywhere in the room and do anything that the music tells them to do.

6. Play a quiet bit of music to allow rest and give the children a sense of contrast.

7. Play music with a strong beat or staccato rhythm and ask the children to clap as they hear it.

Following are suggestions for activities the teacher can use with the above procedure.

Creative Movement

#1

PURPOSE   *Learning to relax*

Materials   One small limp rag doll
                 Recording of slow quiet music.[11]

Procedure   1. Have children sit on the floor around the teacher.
                 2. Teacher holds rag doll with both hands and shows the children how limp it is. She shakes it gently and calls their attention to the way its head, legs, and arms hang loosely.

---

[10] See Gertrude Knight's films: "Building Children's Personalities with Creative Dancing" (Bailey Films, Inc., 6509 DeLongpre Ave., Hollywood, Ca.); "Early Childhood Movement, Dance for Joy" (Documentary Films, 3217 Trout Gulch Road, Aptos, Ca.). Recommended records accompanying the creative movement exercises are among some of the children's favorites in Gertrude Knight's creative dance classes.

[11] "Songs In Spanish For Children" (Columbia 91A02029); "Duets With Spanish Guitar" (Capitol 8406). (Try the different bands to find most suitable mood.)

3. Have children shake their hands and arms and let them hang limp. Do the same with their heads and bodies.
4. Play the record and have children move around the room as if they were like rag dolls.
5. Have children lie down. Go around to each one and lift their arms and legs and let them drop gently, saying:
Feel like a rag doll. Make your arms and legs heavy and floppy.

Creative Movement

#2

PURPOSE   *Learning to stretch*

Materials   Chinese jump ropes
Recordings appropriate for stretching movements[12]

Procedure   1. Demonstrate how the Chinese jump rope stretches.
2. Let each child have a jump rope.
3. Say:
Show me how you can stretch this rope with your hands and arms.
Show me another way you can do it (holding rope with foot and stretching with the arm; holding with both feet; holding rope around various parts of the body).
4. Play the recording and ask children to stretch to the music.
5. Suggest long slow movements.
6. Collect the ropes and continue to play the music.
7. Say:
Now stretch to the music. Stretch all parts of yourself. Stretch your arms, stretch your legs, stretch your body as you move to the music (teacher should stretch along with the children).
Remember how it felt when you were pulling the ropes? Stretch as if you were still pulling on the rope.
Stretch your hands up; feel the top of your head reaching the ceiling. Lie on the floor and stretch your fingers and arms and legs. Stretch your fingers as far as possible from your toes.

Creative Movement

#3

PURPOSE   *Learning to move every part of the body*

---

[12] "Natay, Navajo Singer" (Arizona 6160); "Balalaika" (Elektra EKS7194).

HELPFUL HINTS

1. Provide ample space and permission for children to observe.

2. Not everyone has to participate.

3. Invite children with comments like: "We have a place here, Mary"; "We need another dancer"; "You can hold my hand, Jimmy"; "There's room if you decide you'd like to join us later."

Materials   Recordings of both fast and slow music[13]
Small finger puppets

Procedure   1. Have children sit in a circle.
2. Say:
We can dance with many parts of our body. We don't have to use just our feet.
Our fingers can dance too.
3. Demonstrate with the finger puppets.
4. Let each child play with a finger puppet.
5. Play the recording and suggest that the children let their fingers dance to the music.
Say:
Pretend your fingers are candles with flames moving.
Pretend your fingers are sparklers with sparks flying from them.
6. Sitting still, suggest children dance with other parts of their body. Say:

---

[13] "Music of Golden Africa" (Universal DC6485).

Dance with your whole arm.
Move your head to the music
Dance with one arm and your shoulder.
Move just your arms and head.

Creative Movement

#4

PURPOSE *Learning to relate movement to space*

Materials Large and small cardboard containers
Recordings of medium to slow music[14]

Procedure 1. Play the recording and suggest children dance in and around the cartons.
2. Say:
We all need space to move. Move into a small space.
Now use big spaces.
3. Suggest climbing, crawling, hiding in and under various spaces in the room. Tell them to fit into different spaces.
4. Say:
When you are in a small space, you make small movements.
Show me how you moved when you were inside the box.
When you are in a large open space, you can make big movements. Show me how you moved when you had lots of space.

Creative Movement

#5

PURPOSE *Learning to make heavy and light movements*

Materials Balloons, scarves, heavy blocks
Recordings of slow "heavy" music and "light" music[15]

Procedure 1. Ask children to watch how the balloon moves when you toss it in the air. Reach up with stretching movements to grasp the balloon as it comes down.
2. Say:
A balloon is very light. Move like the balloon.
3. Give each child a balloon and comment on the way each one moves and stretches and lifts up on his toes, etc.
4. Phrase the movements that convey the feeling of lightness:
I like the way you bounce so lightly on your feet, John.

---

[14] "Hadjidakis, Lilacs Out Of The Dead Land" (Odeon).
[15] "Shalom" ["Orcha Bamidbar"] band for heavy mood (Elektra EKL146); Geula Gill: "Newest Hits in Israel" (Epic LF18045); "Iron Butterfly [drum part in middle of record] (Atco SD33–250); "Bantu Folk Songs" (Folkways FW6912).

HELPFUL HINTS

Mary, that's a lovely way to move your arms. Your whole body is moving in such a light way.

5. If balloons are too distracting, use scarves.

6. Demonstrate with heavy blocks by having each child move with a block in his hands.

7. Play heavy-sounding music and say:
Move like you are as heavy as a block. Move your feet and arms and body in a heavy way.

8. Contrast both heavy and light and comment as children move to each kind of music:
I see you're putting your whole foot down at once.
You're dragging your shoulders, and your arms and hands are so heavy. Listen to what the music tells you to do.

Creative Movement

#6

PURPOSE   *Learning to relate movements to others*

Materials   Scarves
Chinese jump ropes
Recordings appropriate for dancing and skipping[16]

Procedure   1. Ask children to hold hands with partners and skip.

2. If children can't skip, let those who know how hold hands with those who don't. Skipping-like movements are all right. Practice doing the activity in pairs.

3. Let pairs of children hold hands and skip around the room, trying not to bump.

4. Give a Chinese jump rope or a scarf to each pair of children to share.

5. Play music and say:
It feels different to move with someone else. Show me how you move with your partner using the rope or scarf.

---

[16] "Original Score of Butch Cassidy and the Sundance Kid" (A&M Records SP4227).

6. Keep each pair together and comment on movements which indicate a child is aware of the other child's presence:
I like the way you both move so close to each other without touching.
That's nice the way your back and arms touch while you move and turn to the music.

Bibliography of Resources

Books About Creative Expression for the Teacher

Burton, William H., and Helen Heffernan. *The step beyond: creativity.* Washington, D.C.: National Education Association, 1964. An excellent resource for the teacher covering the general areas of stimulation of creativity for the teacher, theoretical considerations, and major observable levels of the creative process. There is a helpful examination of some of the characteristics of the creative individual and the creative teacher.

Getzels, Jacob W., and Philip W. Jackson. *Creativity and intelligence: explorations with gifted students.* New York: John Wiley & Sons, 1962. This book is an inquiry into the relationship between creativity and intelligence with case histories and detailed comparisons of children with respect to their creativity, I.Q.'s, personal values, and family backgrounds. Highly intelligent children and highly creative children differ significantly.

Gowan, John Curtis, *et al.* (eds.). *Creativity: its educational implications.* New York: John Wiley & Sons, 1967. This is a collection of readings which gives the teacher some insights into the creative potential of children and provides ideas for practical application of research in the curriculum.

Hartley, Ruth E., *et al. Understanding children's play.* (See Books About Art for the Teacher).

Murphy, Gardner. *Human potentialities.* New York: Basic Books, 1958. The author presents a thoughtful discussion about human nature and culture from a twentieth century vantage point. In Part III, his examination of creativity and the freeing of intelligence is a provocative treatment of the topic for the teacher.

Torrance, E. Paul. *Guiding creative talent.* Englewood Cliffs, N.J.: Prentice-Hall, 1962. This is a discussion of creative talent at all ages and educational levels. The author presents information based on research, and gives examples of specific tasks used to assess creativity. He examines some of the difficulties which educators face in understanding and maintaining creativity.

Books About Creative Movement Activities

Andrews, Gladys. *Creative rhythmic movement for children.* Englewood Cliffs, N.J.: Prentice-Hall, 1954. An excellent book for teachers who work with children of any age. The text includes discussions of the various age levels and how the teacher and children learn through creative movement experiences. Chapters include illustrated demonstration lessons and appropriate music accompaniment for exploring space and rhythm. Another chapter provides instructions for making percussion instruments and suggestions about how the children can make sounds with parts of their bodies. The bibliography is helpful in suggesting resources for encouraging creativity in art, dance, dramatics, language arts, etc.

Barlin, Anne, and Paul Berlin. *The art of learning through movement; a teacher's manual for students of all ages.* Los Angeles: Ward Ritchie Press, 1971. A helpful book for exploring movement through involvement in dramatic play, stories, games, spatial awareness. Included are general hints for teaching the activities. Some sections modified for preschoolers. Good format with many photographs by David Alexander.

Carr, Rachel. *Be a frog, a bird, or a tree. Creative yoga exercises for children.* New York: Doubleday, 1973. Children are encouraged to use their imaginations and pantomime in conjunction with exercises. There is a section of helpful guidelines for teaching yoga, accompanied by illustrations and photographs of young children demonstrating the yoga postures. A selection of exercises can be made to suit the abilities of the children.

Cherry, Clare. *Creative movement for the developing child.* Belmont, Ca.: Fearon, 1968. A nursery school teacher's collection of ideas on involving the young child in such activities as creeping, crawling, walking, balancing games, etc.

Ets, Marie Hall. *Talking without words.* New York: Viking, 1968. This story for children shows how people and animals can communicate silently through the use of body language. Good book to use to explore movement expression.

Gray, Vera, and Rachel Percival. *Music, movement & mime for children.* London: Oxford University Press, 1962. A useful book based on British Broadcasting Company Programs for Music and Movement. There are suggested lessons based on time, weight, and space, plus an appendix of music suitable for movement.

Jones, Elizabeth. *What is music for young children?* Washington, D.C.: National Association for the Education of Young Children, 1969. A discussion of how to plan music experiences for the young child. Included are some observations of music experiences in the classroom.

Maynard, Olga. *Children and dance and music.* New York: Charles Scribner's Sons, 1968. This book is for any adult who works with children in music and dance. The author discusses the child in school, at home, as an artist, and a social person; many ideas are offered for integrating the arts into the curriculum.

Sheehy, Emma D. *Children discover music and dance.* New York: Teachers' College Press, Columbia University, 1968. A useful text for the teacher of children of all ages. Included are discussions of the use of singing, instruments, dance, movement, records, etc., in the classroom.

Taylor, Loren E. *An introduction to dramatics for children.* Minneapolis: Burgess, 1965. "Through play a child extends his experience. . . .Through imagination materials take on new meaning as the child gains new concepts through experience." A rationale for the use of dramatics with children in school. Stresses the value of dramatics in learning. Children, not subject matter, are the primary concern of the skilled teacher. This is one of a series including *Informal dramatics for young children* and *Storytelling and dramatization.*

Records About Creative Movement Activities

In addition to the records listed at the end of each activity in the creative movement section, the teacher can write to the following sources for catalogues and information:

Children's Music Center
5373 West Pico Blvd.
Los Angeles, California 90019

Children's Record Guild
27 Thompson Street
New York, N.Y.

Folkways/Scholastic Records
906 Sylvan Avenue
Englewood Cliffs, New Jersey 07632

Sensorimotor Explorations

Body Awareness

#1

PURPOSE   *Learning parts of the body*

Materials   None[17]

Procedure
1. Say:
   Do you know what your body is? It's you from head to toe. It's all of you.
2. Tell the children that you and they are going to play a game. They will touch the part of their body that you name.
3. Work from top to bottom—head, eyes, nose, ears, mouth, chin, neck, shoulders, chest, back, arms, etc.
4. Repeat. Then call parts of body in random order.
5. Ask if anyone would like to be the leader. As the children learn the names for their body parts, they can name the part as they touch it.

---

[17] See Bibliography of Resources at end of this section for records and books useful in enhancing motor explorations.

Body Awareness

#2

PURPOSE | *Learning how the parts of the body move*

Materials | None

Procedure
1. Tell children they are going to play a game about moving parts of their bodies. Have everyone stand up.
2. Ask how they can move their heads. Take note of the different kinds of responses. Repeat them with the children. Ask how children can move their eyes, mouths, necks, shoulders, elbows, chests (move when they breathe), arms, fingers, waists, hips, legs, knees, ankles, toes.
3. Play a game in which teacher says, "Move your ———." Allow children to use their own type of movement.

Cross reference | Conceptualizing, #2, page 34.

Space Awareness

#1

PURPOSE | *Experiencing space in relation to body*

Materials | None

Procedure
1. Ask children to sit on floor and curl up and try to make themselves round as a ball. You might bring a party noisemaker (one that unrolls when you blow it). Ask them to roll up as it does. Go around looking for spaces. Show them where the empty spaces are by patting, e.g., behind calves.
2. Ask children to use more space around them by stretching their arms, then their legs.
3. Ask them how they can use more space behind themselves, to the side.
4. Have them repeat the entire sequence with their eyes closed.
5. This can be varied by having the children start the exercise by lying on their backs or on their sides.
6. Play a game in which the children put one part of their body in relation to another part as teacher suggests, e.g., "Put your arms between your knees."

Space Awareness

#2

PURPOSE | *Experiencing limitations of space*

Materials | Several large cardboard boxes

Procedure

1. Set the boxes on their sides in a circular pattern like a corral. Leave enough room so that the children, when standing in the middle, will have to take at least three steps to reach them.
2. Ask children to walk slowly and stop when they touch the boxes. Ask them to walk back to the middle of the circle.
3. Move the boxes farther out. Have the children walk out again and back. Then ask them if they had more space to move in or less.
4. Ask them to do 2 and 3 above again with their eyes closed.
5. Take the boxes away and ask the children to move out as far as they can until something stops them. Return.
6. Have children sit down. Talk about how sometimes we can change the size of the space around us, sometimes we can't. For example, ask if, when riding in a car there is anyway to change the space (rolling windows down, putting top of convertible down, putting seat of station wagon down). Talk about whether they have more space in their bathroom or their living room, their living room or their front yard or street. Sometimes it feels good to have a small space, e.g., when you are tucked into your bed.

HELPFUL HINTS

Over, Under & Through, *by Tana Hoban (New York: Macmillan, 1973), provides picture presentations of twelve spatial concepts which you can use to reinforce movement exploration activities. Photographs show children crawling through a pipe, leap-frogging over a hydrant, etc.*

Space Awareness

#3

PURPOSE   *Experiencing spatial relationships*

Materials   One chair per child, a table, a group of objects to place on or under chair (dolls, books, cars, blocks)

Procedure
1. Direct each child to take a chair and put it someplace so that he can walk around it without touching someone else.
2. Tell children to walk around their chairs. Ask if they can move around their chairs in another direction.
3. Ask whether they can move around their chairs without walking.
4. Ask if they can get on top of their chairs:
   Who can get in front of his or her chair, behind it, to the side of it?
5. Ask whether they can get under their chairs. (If not, why not?)
6. Ask if they see anything they can get under (table). Let them get under in suitable groups.
7. Ask:
   Do you see anything on top of the table?
   Pick one of those objects and put it on top of a chair.
   Put your objects under the chair.
   Who can think of another place to put their object?

Cross reference   Pre-reading #11, page 30.

Form Awareness

PURPOSE   *Tactually experiencing form*

Materials   Enough boxes to form the outline of a square 3′ × 3′ base with 3′ sides
Enough boxes to outline a triangle with 4′ base and 3′ high walls
Corrugated cardboard 3′ × 12′ to make a circle
Use one or two aides

Procedure
1. Allow one child at a time to get inside the circle and walk around it running his hand on the side so he feels the curve.

2. Let same child get inside the boxes that form the square and walk or skip around running his hand on the side to feel the straight plane and sharp angles. While the first child is doing this another child can start in the circle.
3. Introduce the triangle in the same manner.
4. After everyone has had a chance to experience the shapes until they are satisfied, sit down and talk about how each space felt different. What was different about each one—curves, straight lines, number of angles (corners).
5. Arrange the boxes so each child can be directed to "go in the circle and come out of the square, etc."

Locomotor Skills[18]

#1

PURPOSE

Learning the feeling of direction (up, down, forward, etc.)
Developing strength and coordination

Materials

Drum or whistle

Procedure

1. Have children stand far enough apart so they can put their arms out without touching anyone else. Explain that when you hit the drum (or blow the whistle), this means you want them to stop and listen.
2. Ask:
   Who can jump?
3. As children jump around, watch and comment on each child, asking:
   Can you jump another way? I see you are jumping forward; (backwards, sideways, crouched, etc.). Can you take a big jump towards me? A little jump?
   Can you move a part of your body while you are up in the air? Find someone to jump with.
   How would you jump if you were mad? How would you jump if you were sad? How would you jump into a swimming pool?
6. Use drum to call children's attention to the objectives you have in mind, i.e., different ways of moving in different directions.
7. There is no right or wrong way to move; the goal is to have each child explore a variety of ways.

Variations

Do the same with hopping, walking, tip-toeing, etc.:
Who can hop? Can you hop and change feet? How tall can you make yourself while you hop? Who can walk without touching anyone?

---

[18] A particularly helpful film is "Movement Exploration" (Robert G. Jenson & Layne C. Hackett, Documentary Films, 3217 Trout Gulch Road, Aptos, California 95003).

AN ACTIVITIES HANDBOOK FOR TEACHERS OF YOUNG CHILDREN

Locomotor Skills

#2

PURPOSE   *Learning the feeling of direction (across and over)*

Materials   Large mattress with sturdy box springs (king-size, if possible) covered with tarpaulin or canvas

Procedure   (Allow only one child at a time on the mattress when doing these directed exercises.)
1. Have child jump from one corner of the mattress to the other corner.
2. Suggest that he land on all fours and jump up again.
3. Have the child turn while he is jumping so that he changes direction.
4. Have child land on his seat and bounce up again.
5. Ask him to close eyes and jump from one end of the mattress to the other.
6. Have him roll over and over again from one end of the mattress to the other.

Locomotor Skills

#3

PURPOSE   *Learning the feeling of direction while walking*

> 1. *Teachers sometimes assume that a child who is highly verbal and intellectually above average is also physically well coordinated. This is not necessarily true.*
> 2. *Observe individual children and keep a record of the activities each favors and those each avoids.*
> 3. *Children who need more practice in physical coordination may be resistive, needing firm but gentle guidance from the teacher.*
> 4. *Be supportive of children who need help. Hold the child's hand while he jumps on the balance board, praise him, let him have more turns, protect him from those who are faster and more likely to push him aside. Provide many positive experiences and lots of praise.*

Materials Drum or whistle for teacher to signal children to stop

Procedure
1. Tell children:
   When I hit the drum (or blow the whistle), it means I want you to stop. I'm going to watch how you walk. Show me how you walk.
2. Give directions:
   Show me how slowly you can walk.
   Now show me how fast you can walk.
   See how close to someone else you can walk without touching. Walk taking giant steps. Walk taking small steps. Walk using a lot of space. Walk using a little bit of space.
3. Ask the following questions:
   How can you walk and make noise with your feet? (shuffle, stamp)
   Can you walk and then turn and walk a different direction when I beat the drum twice?
   How would you feel if you were walking to the store to buy candy? How would you walk if you were going someplace you didn't want to go?

Locomotor Skills

#4

PURPOSE *Learning the feeling of direction while running*

Materials Four barrels, large storage cylinders, or boxes
For the teacher: a drum or whistle to signal children to stop

Procedure
1. Find an area (preferably grassy) at least 20′ long for the running distance and wide enough for the children to stand shoulder to shoulder, about an arm's length apart.
2. Before setting up the barrels, ask the children to line up on one side of the grass. The teacher stands at the other side.
3. Ask them to show you how they can run to your side of the grass as you play the drum and stop quickly when the drum stops.

4. Say:
   *Can you run back slowly and not be very tall? Can you run
   quickly and reach to the sky, be as tall as you can?*
5. Set the barrels up in a line with about three feet of space in
   between. If the children need more space, they can run
   around three barrels.
6. Have them run in and out fast, then slowly, moving another
   part of their body along with their feet.
7. Ask:
   *How would an airplane fly around those barrels? Can you
   show me how a train would move around the barrels?
   What else could you be?*

Locomotor Skills

#5

PURPOSE   *Learning to skip*

Materials   Drum for the teacher or sand blocks to mark the rhythm
               Barrels (optional)

Procedure   1. Ask children to show if they know how to skip. If some
                  children can and some cannot, they can all join hands and
                  skip toward you. Those who are learning to skip will receive
                  movement and rhythm cues from those children who can
                  already skip. Children also can do slow step-hop pattern
                  together.
               2. If the children have accomplished the skipping pattern,
                  they can go on to explore the various movement possibilities
                  similar to the sections on jumping, hopping, walking, and
                  running.

Balance

#1

PURPOSE   *Learning to experience directional changes in space*

Materials   A walking board (1′ wide × 8′ long × 2″ thick) supported by
               small saw horses 8″ off the ground

Procedure   (Work with one child at a time. Use a grassy area.)
               1. Say:
                  *Show me how you can walk across the board.
                  Can you walk across touching your heel to your toes?
                  Try walking backwards.
                  Can you walk sideways on the board? Can you go the other
                      way?
                  Show me how you can walk to the middle, turn around, and
                      walk back towards me.
                  How else can you get to the middle and change?*

2. Ask what other ways they can get across the board. (Possibilities include jumping and hopping sideways and backwards, or using different body positions such as squatting, stooping.)

Balance

#2

PURPOSE
Learning to coordinate weight shift, experiencing right and left sides of body

Materials
A balance board (top: 16″ × 16″ × 1″; base: 5½″ × 5½″ × 2″, both wooden)

Procedure
(Work with one child at a time. Use a grassy area.)
1. Show the child the equipment. Say:

AN ACTIVITIES HANDBOOK FOR TEACHERS OF YOUNG CHILDREN

See what happens when you push with your foot on this side of the board?
What hapens when you push the other side with your foot?

2. Ask the child to get up on the balance board. He may need to hold your hands at first in order to keep his balance. Try to keep most of his weight on the board rather than your hands.

3. Ask him to push down on one foot, then the other. The goal is a smooth shifting of weight. He will probably need a good deal of practice before the goal is reached. Singing "See-Saw, Margery Daw" might help the child to develop a smooth, rhythmic pattern of movement.

4. Ask:
   What happens if you lean on your toes? What else could you lean on (heels)?
   Ask him to combine the movements.

5. As the child becomes skilled, you can talk about pushing "forward, backward, and side to side."

Balance

#3

PURPOSE   *Practicing balance, experiencing directional changes*

Materials   For each child: one hula hoop, one red cardboard square
               (8″ × 8″), one red cardboard circle
               For the teacher: one red square, one red circle

Procedure   1. Give each child a hula hoop. Ask children to put it on the ground in a place where they have room to move around it. Ask them to stand behind their hoops, facing you. Call that their "Home" position.

               2. Say:
                  Can you jump into your hoop with both feet? Can you jump out the other side? Turn around and jump back through.

               3. Ask who can hop on one foot into the hoop and hop out the other side. Can they hop back through. Ask them to hop through using their other foot this time.

               4. Ask them to hop into the hoop using both feet and stop. Ask if they can see a place to jump where they haven't been yet (to the side). Have them practice jumping to the side on both feet, on one foot.

               5. Tell them they are going to play a game. Put a circle on the side of the hoop which is to their right; put a square to their left.

               6. Play the game by asking who can jump into the hoop and out onto the circle. Ask them to jump into the hoop and out onto the square, then back again. After the children are aware of the possible bases, encourage them to explore different combinations, i.e., jump in and out toward the teacher and go back and land on the circle. Ask what different way they could go back besides straight to "Home."

1. *Don't expect children to stand still and pay attention after you hand them a ball, a tire, or a hula hoop. Let them experiment with free movements.*
2. *Begin with simple activities and do not end on a failure. Stop the activity when children are still succeeding.*
3. *If the group is large, use a whistle to signal the beginning and ending of an activity.*
4. *Demonstrate what you want before distributing materials.*

Balance

#4

PURPOSE   *Balancing*

Materials   One automobile tire for each child (get used ones free from a service station)

Procedure   1. Give each child a tire.
2. Ask how he can get from one side of the tire to the other side without touching the tire (walk around it, hop into the middle and out).
3. Ask how can he get from one side of the tire to the other by touching the tire (walk around the edge, hop on one edge, jump into the center, jump over the other edge and out, jump around the edge, etc.) Encourage the children to explore all the possibilities offering indirect clues, i.e., by using one foot, by touching twice, etc.

Combining Movements

#1

PURPOSE   *Combining movements*

Materials   Walking board, saw horses, and mattress

Procedure   1. Set up the walking board so that it is at the edge of the mattress. Use a grassy area.
2. Let the children take turns moving across the board in any manner they choose and end by jumping on the mattress. Encourage them to try new movement combinations by saying you like what they are doing. Help them think of new things to do by asking if they can move their hands or whether they can use one foot, etc. Other possible questions are the following:
Can you look somewhere different when you land?
Can you go higher as you move across?

3. Once they land on the mattress they can explore the space available, the movement combinations, and the various body postures.

Combining Movements

#2

PURPOSE   *Combining movements*

Materials   Any or all of the following:
Big wooden blocks (for walking around, jumping over, hopping onto and off of)
4 chairs
2 or more yardsticks (use with chairs or blocks for going over or under)
Walking board
Mattress
Big boxes or barrels
Auto or bicycle tires (for hopping into, running through, walking on)
Chalk for drawing guidelines through the maze
Rope at least 9′ in length
Footprint patterns (see following activity)

Procedure   1. Set up maze.
2. Allow the children to go through the maze any way they want the first time as long as they follow the guideline. Keep the children spaced 15 feet apart.
3. The second time they go through ask them to do something specific at one point, e.g., hop off the blocks.
4. Each time change the point at which they are to do something specific.

Combining Movements

#3

PURPOSE   *Combining movements*

Materials   One sheet of butcher paper (10 feet long) per child
A plastic dishpan with ½″ of easel paint (see pp. 127-8)
2 child-sized chairs
A basin of soapy water
A towel

Procedure   1. Seat the barefooted child on the chair which has been placed at one end of the butcher paper.
2. Have him put his feet in the dish pan of paint. Help him to step onto the paper.

3. Say:

    Show me how you can move on your feet across that paper to the other end. (He may simply walk straight across the sheet.)

4. Have a person at the other end of the paper with the other chair beside the pan of soapy water and a towel. Have child step in, clean his feet, and dry himself off.

5. Note on the paper who walked it and when.

6. As a follow-up the next day or so, show the child his footprints from his first experience; have him walk on the prints. Set up a blank sheet for him and ask him to go across the paper differently than he did before. Should he balk once on the paper, the teacher can guide him by asking, "Can you hop?" Other movement possibilities are jump on both feet, step sideways with one foot or the other, cross one foot in front of the other.

Bibliography of Resources

Books About Sensorimotor Explorations

Bentley, William G. *Learning to move and moving to learn.* New York: Citation Press, 1970. Concisely prepared booklet with simple outlines for movement activities covering such skills as directionality, laterality, axial movements. Designed primarily for elementary-age children, but also useful with preprimary. Selected bibliography and list of related audio visual materials are helpful.

Braley, William T., *et al. Daily sensorimotor training activities: a handbook for teachers and parents of pre-school children.* Freeport, N.Y.: Educational Activities, 1968, A manual designed with activities which can be integrated into the pre-school curriculum. The daily lesson plan of activities progress through a thirty-four week training period. Some of the activities involve body image (directing children to touch body parts as named), space and direction ("Put your arms in back of your legs"), balance, hearing discrimination, form perception, and other such exercises.

Cratty, Bryant J. *Movement, perception and thought, the use of total body movement as a learning modality.* Mt. View, Ca.: Peek Publications, 1969. The author explores activities which involve total body movement and action resulting in the development of certain kinds of concepts. Children with learning difficulties often benefit from the exercises given in the book. For example, one of the exercises in pattern recognition suggests that the child be given a triangle to hold while he walks that same pattern into the sand. Another in number recognition requires that the child looks at a number on the chalk board and then jump onto that same number in a grid of numbers placed on the ground.

———. *Learning and playing, fifty vigorous activities for the atypical child.* Freeport, N.Y.: Educational Activities, 1968. This is a packet of recipe-type cards with activities such as those mentioned above including circle games, rope and grid games, and other tasks which require physical involvement. Each card indicates the age level for which the activity is suited.

Ferraiuolo, Jerd. *First fitness.* Palo Alto, Ca.: Products of the Behavioral Sciences, 1968. This booklet is based on the premise that there is a high correlation between physical abilities of children and their scholastic achievement. The goals for the fitness program outlined are to help the child increase his awareness of body image, left-right perception, laterality, and other visual motor skills. Some of the activities may be too difficult for the pre-schooler, but the teacher can adapt many of the balance and circle games for use in the nursery school.

Glass, Henry ("Buzz"). *Exploring movement.* Freeport, N.Y.: Educational Activities, 1966. This booklet provides the teacher with many activities on movement exploration such as leaping, clapping, twisting, etc., and using the child's imagination to involve him in participation.

Hackett, Layne C. *Movement exploration and games for the mentally retarded.* Mt. View, Ca.: Peek Publications, 1970. The activities presented in this booklet are non-competitive; they are child-centered and provide successful experiences. For example, the tasks call for asking children to show "how far you can reach with your hands" or "how you can put your heels together" instead of fostering competition among the children. Most of the activities are designed for older children, but the teacher can use them as a basis for adapting the ideas to suit her own needs.

————, and Robert G. Jenson. *A guide to movement exploration.* Mt. View, Ca.: Peek Publications, 1967. The movement exploration activities are designed for the elementary school child but can be adapted for the pre-schooler. These tasks allow the child to develop and progress at his own rate and include helpful teaching techniques.

Porter, Lorena. *Movement education for children.* Washington, D.C.: American Association of Elementary-Kindergarten-Nursery Educators, 1969. This booklet is designed for an elementary school physical education program, but the emphasis on helping the child to learn how to control his body through physical activities is useful for teachers of all ages. There is a helpful bibliography of publications and films included.

Records About Sensorimotor Explorations

Children's Music Center, 5373 West Pico Blvd., Los Angeles, Ca., 90019, has an excellent selection of records and books dealing with "Self and Body Image." Some of these include songs like "My Body," "Put Your Finger in the Air," "Touch and Say Different Parts of the Body," etc.

Educational Activities, Inc., Freeport, N.Y. 11520, distributes a series of records by Hap Palmer dealing with "Learning Basic Skills Through Music." The three volumes contain songs titled "High and Low," "Walk Around the Circle," "Colors," "One Shape, Three Shapes." Another series by Dorothy Carr, "Basic Concepts Through Dance" teaches body image and position in space with tunes like "Hokey Pokey," "Bunny Hop," "Hitch Hiker," etc.

Part 4 / Pre-Math Experiences

Introduction

Mathematical concepts can be incorporated into every area of the curriculum. It is not necessary to sit a child down and "teach him math" at a specific time each day. The young child learns concepts underlying mathematical operations in many of his daily activities: one-to-one relationships as in "one trike for Jimmy, one for John, one for me, and none left for Alan to ride."

Numbers are all around. It is *3* o'clock, *five* children can go to the store, *two* cups of flour are needed for the recipe, there are *two* children in the sandbox," etc. Numbers are part of songs and stories.

The child learns to recognize geometric shapes—the circle of a clock face, the rectangular table, the square blocks. In a grocery store, the children learn about money and perhaps even the concept of making change in simple transactions.

In cooking activities, children learn sequence and how quantities are related. "You put the flour in first, the sugar second, and the baking powder in last. Three teaspoons equal one tablespoon," etc.

The child learns from his daily experience; the wise parent and the experienced teacher will use these moments and events to teach the child about the world in which he lives.

Some of the tasks included here may seem simple, but the teacher should be cautious that she does not assume too much. For example, a child who knows how to count from one to ten does not necessarily understand the concept of numbers and what they stand for. Very often a child will say "I can count to ten" and proceed to do so correctly, but place seven objects in front of him and ask him to count them and he may point to each object and still count to ten. The tasks described here are primarily for the child but they should also help the teacher and parent assess the level of a child's logical understanding of number concepts rather than his rote memory of terminology.

Teachers are sometimes apprehensive at the prospect of teaching the "new math" which students are expected to learn in many elementary schools in the United States. They need not be so concerned; once the teacher and child become familiar with the vocabulary of the new math techniques, the terms become easier to use. The concepts to be taught are very much the same as in years past, but the terminology has changed.

The terms below are designed to encompass a large idea into a word or few words. Use them and become comfortable with them. The ideas involved prepare the foundation for logical concepts to be used later.

Terms	Definitions
Cardinal	The names of the numbers or the counting numbers. They tell us *how many.* Examples: *one, five, fifty;* he has *two* hands and *ten* fingers.
Ordinal	Numbers which tell us *which one* and express succession in a series. Examples: *First, last, second, tenth.* The *fifth* child in the *first* row.
Comparison of Numbers	When numbers are in sequence, such as 1.2.3.4.5, then 5 is greater than (>) 3 3 is less than (<) 5
Pairing or Matching	One to one correspondence. When one set is equal to another. Or, when one set has the same number of members as another set. Examples: 2 beads and 2 blocks or □□ and △△
Set	A collection of things. Things belonging to a set are its members or elements. A set may have many or few members, or *no* members (empty set). Example: members of the class = a set.
Subset	A set within a given set. Examples: Set = members of the class. Subset = members of the class with brown shoes.
Comparison of Sets	*More than* and *fewer than* are the words used in comparing sets. *Are there more members in this set than in that set? Which set has fewer members?* □□□□ △△ (more than) (fewer than) This concept is taught more easily after *pairing,* and *more than* is more easily grasped than the concept *fewer than.*

Conservation of
Quantity

The quantity of matter remains constant no matter what shape it assumes.

Preschool equipment can be adapted for use in the pre-math program. The following list illustrates the types of concepts that can be developed through the use of specific equipment:

Equipment	Math Concept
1. Blocks	order, sequence, pairing, set, subset, conservation, geometric forms
2. Cuisenaire rods (small wooden rods of different lengths)	comparison, set, subset, conservation, pairing, and matching
3. Puzzles	set, subset, conservation
4. Dominoes	cardinality, sequence
5. Geometric shape puzzles, and Parquetry blocks	set, subset, conservation
6. Clocks	sequence, comparison of numbers
7. Tape measures, rulers	cardinality, sequence, comparison of numbers
8. Calendars	sequence, comparison of numbers, cardinality
9. Measuring cups and spoons	comparison of numbers, conservation of quantity
10. Wooden cylinders	comparison of sets, conservation of quantity

Mathematical Vocabulary

The understanding of mathematical concepts begins with a vocabulary that provides young children with the necessary terms and symbols to communicate and label their experiences.

The teacher can plan activities to include experiences with some of the following terms:

Number	Sets
some	alike
a few	as many as
a lot	subset
first, second, etc.	order
greater than	different
less than	join
position	member
zero	pair
	equivalent
	collection

Comparison

big, bigger, biggest
few, fewer, fewest
great, greater, greatest
large, larger, largest
less, lesser, least
little, littler, littlest
many, more, most
small, smaller, smallest
thick, thicker, thickest
thin, thinner, thinnest
same, different

Position

above, below
before, after
in front of
in back of
top, center, bottom
high, low
around, behind
inside, outside
up, down
far, near
here, there

Measurement[1]

Time

morning
afternoon
evening
night
day
soon
week
tomorrow
yesterday
early
late
a long time ago
minute
second
new
old

Temperature

hot, cold
thermometer
warm, cool
centigrade
Fahrenheit
Celsius

Liquid

cup
pint
quart
gallon
ounces
milliliter
kiloliter
litre

Linear

foot
inch
yard
kilometer
metre
centimeter
long, longer,
    longest
short, shorter,
    shortest
narrow, wide
measure
tall, taller, tallest
length
width
distance

Speed

faster, faster than
fastest
slow, slower than
slowest

Weight

heavy, light
heavier than,
    lighter than
heaviest, lightest
ounces
pounds
grams
kilograms
milligrams

---

[1] Since the United States will be converting to the metric system, it would be wise for the teacher to acquaint the children with proper terms. Send 55¢ to the Supt. of Documents, U.S. Government Printing Office, Washington, D.C. 20402 for a Metric Chart (C 13.10; 304).

Write also to Metric Information Office, National Bureau of Standards, Washington, D.C. 20234.

Pre-Math Activities

Numbers

#1

CONCEPT   *Names of the cardinal numbers*

Materials   Flannelboard with 5 pieces cut as △ △ △ △ △

Procedure
1. Have objects arranged horizontally.

    △ △ △ △ △

    Count: 1, 2, 3, 4, 5 with children.
2. Rearrange vertically.

    Count again: 1, 2, 3, 4, 5.
3. Rearrange objects:

    Count again (left to right); 1, 2, 3, 4, 5.

Incidental opportunities for teaching concept
1. Teach the song "Ten Little Indians."
2. Count the number of toys in the doll corner, painting corner, sandbox, etc.
3. Count the number of people present—boys, girls, adults.
4. Bounce a ball and call on a child to clap his hands the same number of times. Child who does this correctly becomes the leader. Use drum beats if child has difficulty bouncing a ball.

Numbers

#2

CONCEPT   *Cardinal numbers*

Materials   *At juice time*—chairs, crackers, people

Procedure
1. Have children sit at juice table.
2. Count the number of chairs, crackers, people, with the children.
3. Hold up four fingers and ask the children to count how many there are.
4. Hold up your fingers in a different combination (e.g., two fingers of each hand) and ask if that is the same number.

5. Change combinations in presenting a number concept to be certain children understand numbers logically.

Numbers

#3

CONCEPT   *Cardinal numbers*

Materials   Egg carton
12 plastic eggs, all the same color (the kind that is hollow and screws open)
1 larger hollow plastic egg
Objects suitable for counting, such as buttons, styrofoam packing materials, Cheerios, etc.

Procedure   1. Use felt pen to number each egg from 1 to 12. Make the same number of dots on each egg to correspond to the number.
2. Place any number of eggs in the carton, depending on the ability of the child.
3. Place uniform counting materials in large egg.
4. Have child place correct number of buttons (or Cheerios, etc.) in egg to correspond to the number indicated.
5. Be sure to check for correct counting after each series.
6. As the child becomes more capable, add different numbers and mix the eggs up.
7. Addition and subtraction problems can also be carried out in the same way.

AN ACTIVITIES HANDBOOK FOR TEACHERS OF YOUNG CHILDREN

HELPFUL HINTS

> 1. *Help children become conscious of numbers: count the number of children at each table; count napkins, cups, eating utensils, etc.*
> 2. *Send number tasks home with each child and suggest that family members help to reinforce the teaching of concepts.*
> 3. *Write out numbers in each child's life: his age, address, phone number, number of people in his family, in his school.*

Numbers

#4

CONCEPT | *Cardinal numbers*

Materials | Dice
Pebbles, play coins, or other uniform small objects

Procedure | 1. Have children take turns throwing dice.
2. Let child count the number and take equal number of pebbles or objects from the "kitty."
3. With very young children, use only one die or make a wooden cube with a low number of dots painted on.
4. Have children count out loud.

Variation | 1. Cut out or mark spaces on tagboard.
2. Have child throw dice and move his marker the equivalent number of spaces, making certain he is counting correctly and moving one space for each number.

Numbers

#5

CONCEPT | *Ordinal numbers*

Materials | Four bean bags

Procedure | 1. Have four children in a group.
2. Give a bean bag to each child.
3. Say:
How many bean bags are there?
Let's count them: 1, 2, 3, 4.
If you all throw them, could I catch them all at once?
 (No.)
We could take turns. (Give each child a number.)
You are first; you are second; you are third; and you are fourth. We will throw them in that order. Let's say your numbers together: first, second, third, fourth.

4. Have children throw bags in order.
5. On another day, also ask:
   Who was first, second, third, etc.?

Numbers

#6

CONCEPT   *Ordinal numbers*

Materials   Four paper cups, labeled 1st, 2nd, 3rd, and 4th
             Button

Procedure   1. Place four cups on a table.
             2. Have children close their eyes while a button is hidden under one of the cups.
             3. Have children open their eyes and guess which cup the button is under. (Child must say "The button is under the [first, second, third, fourth] cup," and not simply point or say "that one.")
             4. Label and add more cups as children learn their ordinal numbers.

Numbers

#7

CONCEPT   *Ordinal numbers*

Materials   Blocks or other common objects

Procedure   1. Begin with a group of four children and four blocks.
             2. Say:
                Let's count the blocks (1, 2, 3, 4). There are four blocks. I will give each of you a block in a certain order. You will be first (give block to a child), *you are second,* (give block to another child), *you are third, etc.*
             3. Have the children repeat "first, second, third, fourth" together. Point to or touch each child as he is labeled.
             4. Say:
                Now I would like you to return the blocks to me in order: first, second, third, fourth.
             5. Increase size of group as children indicate their understanding of the concept.
             6. Children should be grouped according to their ability.

Numbers

#8

CONCEPT   *Ordinal numbers*

Materials	Box filled with matching pairs of items, such as bottle caps, buttons, spools, marbles, small toys
Procedure	1. Place seven non-matching items in a row. This row will serve as a model. 2. Ask child to select matching items and copy the model, making certain that his row is at least 10 inches away from the model. 3. Help child order his items in the same way the model is ordered. 4. Have child verbalize the label, e.g., "The first item is a marble, the second item is a button, the third item is a bottle cap," etc.

Numbers

#9

CONCEPT	*Ordinal numbers*
Materials	Record player and records, or piano, or some other form of musical accompaniment
Procedure	1. Have small group of children line up. 2. Say: *We're going to play a game called "Jumble Up."* *I will give each of you a number in order.* (Assign ordinal number to each child—first, second, third, etc.) *When the music starts, I want you back in the right order.* 3. Play the music and have children move around and get "jumbled up." 4. Stop the music and ask the children to get back in order. When children are back in line, have them repeat the original order as you point to them ("I am first." "I am second," etc.) 5. Number of children and length of time music is played should depend on abilities of children.
Variation	Children can remain "jumbled up" when the music stops and can wait until the teacher calls out, "first, second, third," etc. before taking their places.

Numbers

#10

CONCEPT	*Ordinal numbers*
Materials	Magazine pictures showing sequence of events, cut out from magazine

Photographs of children showing sequence of experiences familiar to them
Drawings of experiences in sequence
File box

Procedure

1. Have each sequence of pictures in separate folder or envelope in the file.
2. Let children work in small groups or separately.
3. Have them sort the pictures into proper sequence.
4. Have them tell what happened *first, second, third.*

Numbers

#11

Concept

Comparison of numbers

Materials

Flannelboard with different shapes cut from construction paper
♡ ♡ ♡ ♡ and ◇ ◇

Procedure

1. Have children stand or sit near flannelboard.
2. Say:
   Are there as many ◇'s as ♡'s?
   Which set has more? How many ♡'s? How many ◇'s?
   The set of 4 is greater than the set of 2.
   We say that 4 is greater than 2.
3. Let each child take a turn manipulating and demonstrating *greater than* and *less than.*

Numbers

#12

Concept

Comparison of numbers

Materials

Five bean bags (or other common objects)

Procedure

1. Have children in groups of a convenient size.
2. Say:
   Let's count the bean bags together. (As you count, push the bean bags aside) *1, 2, 3, 4, 5 bean bags. Which is greater—5 bean bags or 3 bean bags? 5 is greater than 3.*
3. Use other objects such as buttons or beads; use amounts which are greater than, or less than.

Incidental opportunities for teaching concept

1. Count children as they sit down at the juice table.
2. Count the steps involved in getting dressed.
3. Count the steps involved in doing an art project: first, cut; second, paste; third, color.

4. In a cooking activity, point out the order in which ingredients are added.
5. Use appropriate stories, such as *The Three Bears* or *Caps For Sale* to give practice in repeating ordinal numbers.
6. Ask a child to assign the correct number of children to a particular number of chairs.
7. Sing "Ten Little Indians." Have the children say which is greater: three Indians, two Indians, four Indians, etc.
8. Compare ages of grandmother, mother, child. Which is greater?

Forms

#1

CONCEPT *Geometric forms*

Materials Geometric forms cut from construction paper ○ □ △ ▭
Paper clip attached to each form
Pole (more than one, if possible)
Magnet attached to pole with string

Procedure 1. Spread forms on the floor.
2. Hold up a shape (△) and ask child to "fish" for a shape that matches.
3. Let child fish for shape; when he finds it, ask the name of the shape.
4. Hold up another shape, and ask another child to fish for that shape. Repeat until each child has had a chance to fish.

Forms

#2

CONCEPT *Geometric forms*

Materials Large assortment of each of four shapes: triangle, circle, square, rectangle
Box divided into four equal compartments
Example of one of the shapes pasted on each of the compartments

Procedure 1. Mix all shapes together on a table.
2. Have child sort forms into appropriately labeled compartments, naming the forms as he sorts them.

Variations 1. Use large and small shapes.
2. Use shapes of different colors.

> 1. *Have the children help make a large poster of different shapes and label them. Post the names of the children who can identify each of the shapes.*
> 2. *Cut sandwiches, cookies, and snacks into geometric shapes and talk about shapes as children eat.*
> 3. *Cut sponges into different shapes and use for making paint designs on construction paper.*

3. Have the child sort shapes in any way he chooses. Have him tell why he categorized in the way he did. Most young children will sort according to color, then shape, and finally size.

Forms

#3

CONCEPT   *Geometric forms*

Materials   Flannelboard with at least two cutouts of each of the four shapes used in Forms #1 and #2

Procedure
1. Place a △ on the flannelboard.
2. Say:
   Who can find a shape to match this one? (Let child find it.)
3. Repeat the same procedure with each shape.
4. Let the children then pick a shape and choose a friend to find a matching shape.

Forms

#4

CONCEPT   *Geometric forms*

Materials   Cards of heavy tagboard, each made like a grid with different shapes in each square
Cutout cardboard shapes to match

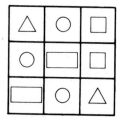

Procedure
1. Have children place matching shapes on the card.
2. Have children name the shapes as they select them.

3. Or, have children take turns drawing shapes from a box. As each child pulls a shape out, he places it in the appropriate square. If he has no square left to cover, he may choose to give it to another child who needs that particular shape.
4. Or, each child can be given a handful of shapes and the teacher or another child draw shapes from a box, calling them out as in Bingo.

Forms

#5

CONCEPT   *Geometric forms*

Materials   Wooden ¾ inch thick board, 12 inches square
25 nails, 1 to 1¼ inches long
Box of rubber bands

Procedure   1. Hammer the nails into (but not through) the board in a 5 × 5 array.
2. Use a rubber band to make a square shape and ask the children to make a shape just like the one you made.
3. Do the same with triangle and rectangle.
4. Name each shape as you make it.
5. Let children experiment with the shapes they can make and help them make them.

Variation	The form board can also be made with golf tees glued into a peg board.
Incidental opportunities for teaching concept	1. Construct shapes with yarn or tape. 2. Mark geometric shapes on the floor with chalk or tape and have children singly or in a group reproduce those shapes with their bodies by lying on top of them. 3. Have children look around the room for shapes in the windows, doors, chairs, bookcases, blocks, balls, musical instruments, etc. 4. Use geometric shapes to distribute to children at dismissal time or transition time: *The children with triangles may go to juice time.* *The children holding circles may get ready to go home.* 5. Cut sandwiches into geometric shapes at lunch time. Identify the shapes. Have children bite their cookies or sandwiches into other shapes and name them.

Pairing and matching

#1

Concept	*Pairing and matching sets*
Materials	Assorted pairs (sets) of objects such as 2 forks and 2 crayons, 2 scissors and 2 pencils, 2 paper clips and 2 safety pins
Procedure	1. Have children in 3 small groups at a table. 2. Say to the first group: *Here is a set of forks and a set of crayons. Let's count the members in each set (2). Are they the same in each set? (Yes.) Then we say that they are pairs. The sets match. Each one has the same number of members.* 3. Say to second group: *Here is a set of scissors and a set of pencils. Let's count the members in each set (2). Are they the same? (Yes.) Then we can call them pairs. Each set has the same number of members.* 4. Do the same for third group.

Pairing and Matching

#2

Concept	*Pairing and matching groups of objects*
Materials	Flannelboard Cut-outs of three different colored pigs, three kinds of houses (straw, twig, brick with a chimney), and three arrows
Procedure	1. Tell the story of "The Three Little Pigs" emphasizing which

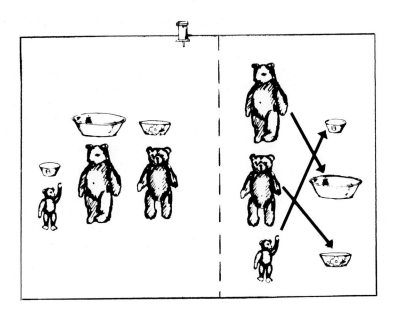

🖊 pig goes with which house and using the arrows to point to the correct pairing.

2. When the children are familiar with the pairing, mix the houses and pigs and let them use the arrows to indicate which pig matches with which house.

Variation   Use cut-outs of "The Three Bears" and different size chairs, bowls, beds, etc.

Pairing and Matching

#3

CONCEPT   *Pairing and matching two sets*

Materials   Flannelboard with enough objects cut out to pair, at least 3 each of the following shapes: ⊕ ○ ♡ △

Procedure   1. Have children in a convenient group around the flannelboard. Take two ⊕'s and two ♡'s
2. Say:
Are there more crosses or more hearts?
3. Rearrange in two similar groups of three, e.g.:
   △△△   ♡♡♡
4. Ask if the sets match. Do they have the same number of members?
5. Arrange in unlike (dissimilar) sets. Say:
Do these match? They are pairs because they have the same number of members.

   △♡○   ⊕○△

Pairing and Matching

#4

CONCEPT   *Pairing and matching more than two sets*

Materials   Flannelboard and cutouts used in Pairing and Matching #2

Procedure   1. Place groups of different shapes on the flannelboard:

      ○ ○ ○   ♡ ♡

      △ △ △ △ △   □ □ □

2. Say:
Who can show me the sets that match? Come and make a ring around them. Why do they match? (Because these groups have the same number of objects.)

3. Make other combinations. Have children come to the flannelboard and circle the matching sets:

(○○)   (□□)   ✛ ✛ ✛   ♡ ♡ ♡ ♡

Pairing and Matching

#5

CONCEPT   *Pairing and matching sets with unequal members*

Materials   Flannelboard with cutouts used in previous lessons

Procedure   1. Have children in group around you.

2. Say:
Here are two sets: △ △   ♡ ♡

Let's count the members in each of these sets. Are they the same? (Yes.)

3. Arrange 2 more sets: □ □   ○ ○

4. Say:
Let's count the members. Are they the same? (Yes.)

5. Rearrange so that the sets are unequal. □ □ □   ○ ○

6. Say:
Let's count the members again. Are they pairs? (No.) *Why not?* (Because they have different numbers of members.)

7. Do as often as necessary to teach matching concept.

Pairing and Matching

#6

CONCEPT   *Equivalence*

Materials	Collection of buttons or other easily manipulated objects, all uniform in size and shape, but in two colors, e.g., black buttons and white buttons
Procedure	1. Give child a handful of buttons (about 12).
	2. Teacher should take a handful of the opposite color.
	3. Make a row of 6 buttons equally spaced.
	4. Ask child to make a row just like yours with his buttons.
	5. If the child does not have the concept of one-to-one correspondence, he is likely to use all his buttons or make a row which is not equivalent, though the two end buttons may match.
	6. After each trial, change the number of buttons.
	7. Give the child many opportunities to learn through manipulation about one-to-one correspondence.
Incidental opportunities for teaching concept	1. Have children set the table matching correct number of napkins, cups, etc. to the number of chairs.
	2. During stories or music time, have children close their eyes and listen while the teacher claps her hands three times. Have children open their eyes and clap their hands the same number of times. Increase in number and variety of patterns.
	3. Match ordinary items, like paint brushes to containers of paint, coats to children, etc.

Pairing and Matching

#7

CONCEPT	*Equivalence*
Materials	Flannelboard

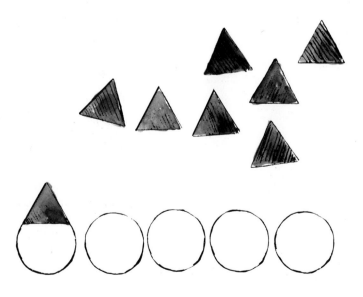

Ten or more circles to represent heads
Ten or more cone shapes to represent hats

Procedure
1. Place a circle on the flannelboard and say:
   This is a head and I want to put a hat on it. (Place a cone on top of the circle.)
2. Place another circle on the board and say:
   Here is another head.
3. Continue to place circles on board and ask:
   How many hats do we need?
   (If children begin to guess, ask:
   How can we find out?)
4. Let each child show how he understands pairing.
5. Let each child pick up (or count out) the number of hats he thinks he will need each time you put up a series of circles.
6. Do not correct and teach the child; rather, watch how he tries to figure out the problem. Children who do not understand equivalence need to be given many opportunities to do pairing and matching activities.

Comparisons

#1

CONCEPT   *More than, fewer than*

Materials   Set of blocks

Procedure
1. Have children count the blocks with the teacher.
2. Teacher then distributes varying numbers of blocks to each child, counting each block as she hands it to the child. Example:
   I am giving John one block, two blocks, three blocks. Now I am giving Jane one block, two blocks. I wonder who has more? Let's count them together. John has more blocks than Jane. There are more blocks in John's set. Jane has fewer than John.
3. Vary in difficulty according to the abilities of the children.
4. Similar comparisons can be made with equipment and toys in all other areas of the school and home.

Comparisons

#2

CONCEPT   *More than, fewer than*

Materials   Collection of buttons or similar objects, all uniform in color, shape, and size

Procedure
1. Place four buttons on a table in random design.

2. Have children look at the buttons and count them.
3. Have children close their eyes while teacher takes one button away.
4. Have children open their eyes and tell if there are *more* or *fewer* buttons than before.
5. Begin at a level where the children can succeed. Place buttons in a straight line for those who become confused with random design.
6. Increase and vary in difficulty by using more buttons and removing varying numbers, or sometimes leaving the *same* number.

Comparisons

#3

CONCEPT
More than, fewer than

Materials
Container with separate compartments such as an egg carton or muffin tin
Beads for stringing in assorted colors (Be sure the beads have large enough holes so children can string them easily.)
Strings of equal length, knotted at one end and dipped in melted wax at the other end for easier stringing

Procedure
1. Have beads sorted in the compartments according to color.
2. Have children "copy" the teacher's pattern of stringing.
3. Increase difficulty of pattern by adding more colors and more beads, varying the numbers each time. Do not move on to more difficult steps until the children have had many opportunities to indicate they understand the concept.
4. Let children string beads any way they like, but check with each one and have him tell you as he is stringing his beads which are *fewer than* and *more than* and *the same number as*.

Incidental opportunities for teaching concept
1. Compare the number of pieces in two puzzles.
2. Compare the number of boys to the number of girls.
3. Compare color of hair, blonde to brown, etc.
4. Compare room fixtures, windows to doors, lights to doors, etc.
5. Compare foods: crackers and cookies, celery and carrots, etc.
6. Compare stacks of paper juice cups (count numbers in each stack).

Comparisons

#4

CONCEPT
Comparison of numbers

Materials
Cans of varying sizes and shapes: tall, thin, small, wide
Pan full of rice

<table>
<tr><td>Procedure</td><td>

1. Select two cans. Say:
   Which do you think holds the greater amount? (Let children guess.) *How can we find out?*
2. Have child fill one can with rice.
3. Let him pour the rice into the other can.
4. Help him to indicate with words the appropriate concept:
   The green can holds a greater amount of rice than the red can. The blue can holds less than the green can.
</td></tr>
<tr><td>Variation</td><td>

The same activity can be carried on by measuring sand in the sand box or water in the housekeeping area.
</td></tr>
</table>

Sets

#1

<table>
<tr><td>Concept</td><td>Set having like members</td></tr>
<tr><td>Materials</td><td>Sets of objects having like members (blocks, paint brushes, crayons, scissors, etc.)</td></tr>
<tr><td>Procedure</td><td>

1. Have a small group of children at a table or on the floor.
2. Show them one set of like objects (blocks).
3. Say:
   What are these?
   These are all blocks. They belong to a group. This is a group of blocks.
3. Show the children another set of objects. Say:
   What are these? These are all brushes. This is a group of brushes. We can call this a set.
4. Continue with other sets of objects and repeat that each group can be called a *set.*
5. When all objects have been shown, repeat the identification:
   This is a set of blocks.
   This is a set of brushes. Etc.
6. Ask:
   Can you name some other sets in this room? (Help children identify other like objects by the word set.)
</td></tr>
<tr><td>Incidental opportunities for teaching concept</td><td>

1. Use natural experiences of the children to introduce the concept of set. For example, at the juice table, let children help distribute a set of cups. Talk about groups of things that are alike and refer to them as sets. Talk about groups of things that are used for the same purpose and refer to them as sets.
2. Other properties of sets which children can easily recognize are color, size, texture, shape, weight, and length.
</td></tr>
</table>

Sets

#2

<table>
<tr><td>Concept</td><td>Set having unlike members</td></tr>
</table>

Materials	Sets of objects having *unlike* members (sandbox toys, playhouse dress-ups, cooking utensils, equipment used in the art corner)
Procedure	1. Have small group of children on the floor in some other convenient group.

2. Say:
Here are a strainer, eggbeater, spoon, and measuring cup. What are these things used for? (Cooking.)
Are they all alike? (No) *But they are all used for cooking. They are all members of the same set that we will call the "cooking set."*

3. Do the same for each group that you have. Finish by saying:
We will call these members of the same set the _____ *set.*

Sets

#3

CONCEPT	*Subsets*
Materials	Large assortment of buttons
Procedure	1. Have a group of children seated at a table.

2. Distribute a handful of buttons to each child, saying:
Here is a <u>set</u> *of buttons for Mary, here is another* <u>set</u> *of buttons for John, and a* <u>set</u> *of buttons for Jim, etc.*
3. Take a handful of buttons for display purposes.
4. Sort buttons and indicate what you are doing:
I am sorting the red buttons and putting them here. This is my <u>subset</u>. *These red buttons are a* <u>subset</u> *of my buttons.*
5. As the children sort their buttons, reinforce the concept of subset:
I see John is sorting his blue buttons into a separate pile. I wonder if someone knows what we call that pile of buttons?

Incidental opportunities for teaching concept

1. Story Time: Discuss the fact that everyone is a *member of the class.* Have all the children with brown shoes on stand up. They are the *brown shoes subset.* Have all the girls stand up. They are the *girls subset.* Select other qualities familiar to the children, such as color of hair, style of clothing, etc.

2. Juice time: Refer to a basket of crackers as a *set;* each child is given a *subset* of crackers. Do the same with napkins, cups, other objects to reinforce the concept.

3. Music time: If children remove their shoes for dancing, have them place all their shoes together and discuss the fact that these constitute a *set* of shoes. The brown shoes are a *subset.* Let the children determine other ways to establish subsets, such as tennis shoes, sandals, oxfords, etc.

1. *Provide large containers such as dishpans, buckets, sandtables filled with fine-grain sand, rice, flour, water; and measuring utensils, such as measuring spoons, sifters, scales, plastic measuring cups with ounces as well as milliliters marked on them. Talk about pouring, measuring, sifting, comparing, and use words provided in the mathematical vocabulary (see pages 155–156).*
2. *Have children pour different kinds of materials, such as beans, gravel, liquids, etc., from a small to a larger measuring cup, then from the large to the smaller cup. Discuss weight and conservation of quantity (more, less, same).*

Conservation

#1

CONCEPT   *Conservation of quantity (size and color)*

Materials   Flannelboard with cutouts of 2 different sizes and 2 different colors, arranged at random

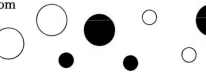

Procedure   1. Have children rearrange the cutouts according to size.
2. Ask children how the cutouts can be arranged another way (by color).

Conservation

#2

CONCEPT   *Conservation of quantity (shape)*

Materials   Assorted shapes (can be of different colors and sizes) arranged at random on flannelboard

Procedure   1. Have children around flannelboard. Say:
How can we group these together in another way? (by shape)
2. Have children regroup them.

Conservation

#3

CONCEPT   *Conservation of quantity (number)*

Materials   Flannelboard
Cutouts of same size and shape, but 2 different colors (e.g., black, white)

Procedure

1. Place six black circles in a row.
2. Have a child place an equal number of white circles in a row beneath the black ones.
3. Pick up the black circles and place them farther apart in a row.

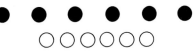

4. Ask:
   Is this the same number (pointing to the black) *as this?* (pointing to the white)
5. Use other arrangements to be certain the child is not using space as basis for his judgment.

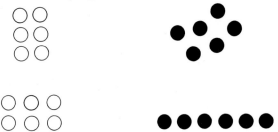

Conservation

#4

CONCEPT   *Conservation of quantity (number)*

Materials   Egg carton
               Black and white beads

Procedure

1. Place one black bead in each of the six compartments on one side of the egg carton.
2. Ask a child to count the number of beads.
3. Pick up one of the beads from a compartment and place it in an adjoining compartment.
4. Ask the child:
   Now are there the same number of beads?
5. If he answers correctly, place six white beads on the other side of the egg carton, one bead in each compartment (*the teacher's side*). *Ask:*
   Do I have the same number of beads as you have?
6. Pick up two of the white beads and place them in adjoining compartments. Ask:
   Now do I have the same number as you have?
7. Vary the location of beads to be certain the child understands the concept of conservation.
8. Add an extra bead and ask:
   Now do I have the same number as you have?

Incidental opportunities for teaching concept

1. With groups of children, regroup according to the suggestions of the class: hair color, color of shoes, boys, girls, etc.

2. Take four or five blocks and arrange them in a row; then stack them. Explain that it is the same quantity each time.
3. Have two groups of children (five in each). Have one group form a circle, and one group sit in a straight line. Point out that each group has the same number.
4. Make different shapes from pieces of heavy string or yarn of equal lengths.

Bibliography of Resources

Resource Materials and Books About Math Concepts

The following may be useful to the teacher who wants to adapt additional curricular ideas to the classroom or wants to do some additional reading about instruction in pre-math.

Beberman, Max (ed.) *Young math books.* New York: Thomas Y. Crowell. This is a series of books designed for the young child, covering such concepts as long, short, high, low, thin, wide, circles and other shapes, and weighing and balancing. Some of these books are too difficult for the very young, but others can be adapted or used as resource material for the teacher.

Branley, Franklyn M. *Think metric!* New York: Thomas Y. Crowell, 1972. Conversion to the metric system may cause some problems for adults who are unaccustomed to the International System of Units. Young children should be introduced to the system early, and teachers of young children will find this book a valuable aid. Written and designed for elementary ages, but very helpful for the adult.

Carmichael, Viola S. *Curriculum ideas for young children.* Southern California Association for the Education of Young Children. Los Angeles, 1971, pp. 63–73. These are suggestions for exercises to illustrate weight, size, and shape concepts. It includes a bibliography of children's books and records dealing with these concepts.

Hainstock, Elizabeth G. *Teaching Montessori in the home.* New York: Random House, 1968. This is a very popular book designed for parents who wish to teach Montessori to their children. The activities are grouped according to "practical life exercises," such as folding a napkin, lacing a shoe, naming colors, etc.; "reading and writing exercises" such as working with sandpaper letters and a movable alphabet; and arithmetic exercises (pp. 78–88). Each activity is clearly presented and illustrated in recipe style specifying materials, demonstration, purpose, and control of error.

Lavatelli, Celia. *Early childhood curriculum: a Piaget program.* American Science and Engineering, 20 Overland St., Boston, Mass. This set of materials includes a book, classification kits, number, measurement, and space kits, and seriation kits for use in teaching concepts.

Lorton, Mary Baratta. *Workjobs.* Menlo Park, Ca.: Addison-Wesley, 1972. Photographs demonstrate well-designed activities for an open classroom. Provides the teacher with ideas for development of language, math, and other concepts.

McIntyre, Margaret. Books which give mathematical concepts to young children: an annotated bibliography. *Young children.* Vol. 24, No. 5, May, 1969, pp. 287–91.

McKillip, W. D. and his associates have prepared a number of curricular guides which are available through McKillip at the Department of Mathematical Education, College of Education, University of Georgia, Athens, Georgia 30601. They are: *Counting* (Practical Paper No. 28; Research and Development Center Educational Stimulation, University of Georgia, Athens, Georgia [McKillip, W. D.], August, 1969); *Matching* (Practical Paper No. 10; Research and Development Center Educational Stimulation [McKillip, W. D.], July, 1969); *Patterns* (Practical Paper No. 32; Research and Development Center Educational Stimulation, [McKillip, W. D], December, 1969); *Geometry* (Practical Paper No. 27; Research and Development Center Educational Stimulation, [Mahaffey, M. L.], August, 1969); *Shadow geometry project* (Practical Paper No. 18; Research and Development Center Educational Stimulation, [Robinson, E. G.], June, 1969). These guides describe lessons and procedures for teaching the specific mathematical concepts indicated in the title. The use of shadows and shadow making to teach geometric shapes is especially interesting.

Nuffield Mathematics Project. *I do, and I understand.* New York: John Wiley and Sons, 1967. This first published booklet of the Nuffield mathematics project deals with the rationale for teaching math to young children and discusses many of the problems involved in setting up a classroom in which math instruction can take place. Useful for the teacher who wants to read more generally about math instruction.

———. *Mathematics begins.* New York: John Wiley and Sons, 1967. This is an excellent booklet designed to help young children perceive the patterns and relationships of mathematics. The section devoted to the preschool experience is especially useful in planning projects and activities which provide children with experiences of space, shape, size, matching, measuring, etc.

———. *Pictorial representation.* New York: John Wiley and Sons, 1967. This booklet provides the teacher with ideas about the use of pictures and graphs to communicate and simplify information. Much of the material is suitable for older children, but some can be easily adapted for use with younger children.

San Felipe Kindergarten. *A kindergarten guide for Indian children.* Available through the Commissioner of Indian Affairs, 1951 Constitution Avenue, N.W., Washington, D.C. 20242. This program was created and adapted to serve Indian children. It includes number concepts, counting, sets, geometric shapes, positional relationships, measurement, and basic operation of addition and subtraction.

Sharp, Evelyn. *Thinking is child's play.* New York: E. P. Dutton, 1969. This is a book of forty games based on the work of Piaget stressing learning concepts through manipulation of objects. Each activity is presented in a simple format with purpose, materials, and comments accompanied by illustrations. This book should make it possible for teachers and parents to put into practice and appreciate the impressive research work of Piaget.

Weikart, David P. et al. *The cognitively oriented curriculum. A framework for preschool teachers.* Washington, D.C.: ERIC-NAEYC, 1971. A description of a curriculum based on Piagetian theory. The second half of the book provides helpful guides to activities in teaching classification, seriation, spatial relations, and temporal relations.

See also Conceptual games (matching, sorting, classifying), pages 38–39, and Books about shapes and numbers, pages 53–54.

Part 5 / **Cooking**

Introduction

Cooking in the preschool is a versatile activity that can be used to reach several quite different objectives. It is intrinsically exciting; children love to do things they see adults doing, and cooking offers an opportunity to do something "real." It provides a way for youngsters to feel important and achieve a sense of accomplishment.

But cooking can be more than fun. With the proper selection of recipes and use of materials, it can provide many opportunities for cognitive, social, and cultural learning as well.

The teacher can use cooking to expose children to a variety of sensory and cognitive experiences. Let the children see how the food can change before their eyes—how brittle noodles become soft and slippery after boiling; how an egg becomes hard when it is cooked. Let them *smell* the aroma of foods—bacon frying, apples baking, onions cooking. Provide many opportunities for them to *feel* the different textures of food—the squishiness of bread dough oozing through their fingers, the roughness of nut shells. Teachers can call attention to *hearing* the different sounds of foods—corn popping, the crunch of celery when the children chew on it.

Note the colors, shapes, and sizes of foods—the black, shiny seeds of the papaya next to the bright orange of the fruit; the white of the coconut meat and the rough, hairy brown shell surrounding it.

With guidance and encouragement, the children begin to learn about units of weights and measures—one teaspoon of vanilla, two cups of sugar, a half pound of flour, three drops of food coloring, etc.—and how these units relate to one another—three teaspoons equal one tablespoon, one cup equals half a pint, sixteen ounces equal one pound, etc. They learn to use proper tools to achieve results—measuring cups for liquids, smaller measures for powders, and solids, such as shortening. They also learn meanings of new words—"dice" the carrots, "fold" in the eggs, "grate" the lemon rind.

The children learn to follow step-by-step instructions—why yeast must be added gradually, why the sugar and butter and not the flour and butter are creamed together, why icing is best put on after the cake is cooled. They can watch physical and chemical changes take place—bread rising, whipping cream solidifying into butter, peanuts being ground into peanut butter. They become aware of the need to learn about time—mixing for two minutes, waiting for the timer to ring, looking at the clock to see when the muffins will be ready, etc.

There are also social gains. Through cooking activities, the child learns and feels the importance of sharing in a group project and realizes the need for cooperation. Planning the project, taking turns at stirring and pouring, talking about the ingredients all require individual contributions to a group effort.

Foods and cooking illustrate cultural differences among ethnic groups, and some of the recipes were selected to emphasize these contrasts: Sushi from Japan, southern spoon bread, Chinese steamed rice, Mexican tortillas. Teachers will find food is generally a welcome topic of interest to all the parents in a school and many adults may be very eager to contribute their own "soul food" recipes. This kind of involvement provides opportunities for parents to contribute something unique and worthwhile to the program and makes it possible for the curriculum to incorporate information about a variety of cultural and ethnic backgrounds as well as expose the children to a wider array of food tastes and flavors. Stories and songs can be tied in with the preparation and serving of certain foods to celebrate customs or holidays. Dishes should be planned and selected to fit into a schedule which allows plenty of time for preparation and consumption. Elaborate dishes which require a great deal of adult preparation and much waiting by the children should be discouraged.

Also, good nutrition should be among one of the most important objectives in a cooking program. The teacher has an opportunity to expose children and parents to healthy foods and help to develop good eating habits. Recipes requiring refined sugars and flour, and ingredients with little food value should be shunned. Whenever possible, whole grains should be used, honey instead of sugar, carob instead of chocolate; use recipes calling for molasses and wheat germ, fresh or dried fruits, nuts and seeds—all of these are tasty and healthful. Our attitudes about "good" foods are conveyed to our children. If gooey, high caloric desserts are held out as a special treat, then children will learn to place a premium on these kinds of foods. Healthy eating habits and knowledge about good nutrition are developed early. The preschool years are the best time to start.

Recipes for this section were chosen to allow children to discover and learn through involvement. Whenever possible, projects should be planned and presented so they may do the measuring, pouring, sifting, cracking of eggs, cutting, peeling, kneading, and mixing. This means pre-planning and anticipating the needs of the children. The teacher may find it most useful to measure the dry ingredients in advance and place only the amount needed in front of the children. She may find it less distracting to limit the number of children to certain kinds of activities, selecting those who are more independent to help those who are less experienced. Clean-up should be part of the planning. Children enjoy wiping, sweeping, washing, and they will participate in these activities as readily as in the cooking if the teacher provides for their involvement—having small brooms handy, sponges, aprons and soapy water, a sink or basin the children can reach, etc. The number of servings indicated are child-size portions.

Some helpful suggestions to keep in mind are:

1. Children with food allergies should be identified. Post a list of the names of children who are allergic along with the foods they cannot eat. Some of the more common foods to which preschoolers are allergic are milk and milk products, juices with high acid content (such as orange or grapefruit), chocolate, eggs, and nuts.

2. Be very cautious when serving or preparing foods which might cause choking, especially nuts, raw carrots, celery, and popcorn. Children should always sit down to eat.

3. Limit the number of children to avoid crowding and to allow for adequate participation by each child.

4. Use low work tables and chairs.

5. Use unbreakable equipment whenever possible.

6. Have enough tools and utensils for the children.

7. Do not let children stand on chairs to reach the stove. Adults should do the cooking over the burners. Turn pot handles away from the edge of the stove. Whenever possible, use electric fry pans or pots on a table at the child's level so he can help with the cooking, reminding him that these utensils are hot.

8. Use blunt knives or serrated plastic knives for cutting cooked eggs, potatoes, bananas, etc. Use vegetable peelers only after demonstrating and supervising carefully.

9. Have only the necessary tools, utensils, and ingredients at the work table. All other materials should be removed as soon as they are no longer needed.

10. Pre-plan the steps of the cooking project and discuss plans with the children before beginning. They should be clear about what they are expected to do and what the adults will do before the cooking materials are made available to them.

11. Long hair should be pulled back and fastened; floppy clothing and cumbersome jackets should be removed. Aprons are not essential but helpful.

12. Wash hands before beginning.

13. Inexperienced children should begin with simple recipes requiring little cooking.

14. Allow plenty of time for discussion, looking at, touching, tasting, comparing. Use every step in the cooking project as an opportunity for the children to expand their learning.

Read "Teachers' Guide to Educational Cooking in the Nursery School—An Everyday Affair" by Nancy Ferreira (*Young Children*, Nov. 1973, pp. 23–32). See Play Dough, page 95, to translate cooking measurements to the metric system.

Cooking Activities

Quick Breads

PLAY DOUGH BISCUITS

(Cooked in electric frying pan right at the dough table)
2 cups sifted unbleached white flour
3¾ teaspoons baking powder
1 teaspoon salt
⅓ cup oil
¾ cup milk
Let children measure and sift dry ingredients. Stir in liquids and mix lightly. Using as little flour as possible on table top, let children knead and roll out dough about ¼ inch thick. Cut to any desired size or shape. Cook in lightly greased electric fry pan on top of table. Heat should be low. Let biscuits brown and raise. Turn and cook on other side. (Packaged refrigerated biscuits also cook up nicely.) Children will tend to overhandle the dough at first, but soon learn to knead lightly. Makes about 20 small biscuits.

QUICK BREAD

Preheat oven to 375°
3¾ cups whole wheat flour
¼ cup wheat germ
1 cup molasses
2 cups buttermilk or yogurt
2 teaspoons soda
pinch of salt
raisins and nuts (optional)
Mix all ingredients together. Bake in one large or several small greased loaf pans for 30 to 40 minutes.

GRAHAM CRACKERS

Preheat oven to 350°
½ cup butter
⅔ cup brown sugar
2¾ cup graham flour
½ teaspoon salt
½ teaspoon baking powder
¼ teaspoon ground cinnamon
Cream butter and sugar well. Mix remaining ingredients and add to creamed mixture, alternating with ½ cup water. Mix well and let stand 30 minutes. Roll out dough on floured board to ⅛ inch thickness. Cut into 2-inch squares and place on greased cookie sheet. Bake for 20 minutes. Makes about 3 dozen.

HELPFUL HINTS

> 1. *Keep cooking activities simple. Shelling peas, shucking corn, and washing vegetables are educational and fun.*
> 2. *Help children plant a vegetable garden to provide food for cooking projects.*
> 3. *Avoid prepackaged, convenience type foods; use recipes that call for natural, unrefined ingredients.*
> 4. *Experiment with substituting honey for sugar; whole grains for refined flour.*
> 5. *Read books on good nutrition.*
> 6. *Serve cheese, raw vegetables, and fresh fruits for snacks.*

BROWN BREAD

Preheat oven to 400°
³/₄ cup flour
1¹/₄ teaspoon soda
³/₄ teaspoon salt
1 cup finely crushed graham cracker crumbs
3 tablespoons shortening
1 egg
1 cup buttermilk (or 1 cup milk with 1 teaspoon vinegar or lemon juice)
¹/₂ cup molasses
¹/₂ cup raisins
Sift flour, soda, and salt. Add graham cracker crumbs. Blend in shortening until texture is like meal. In a separate bowl mix remaining ingredients; combine with dry mixture. Spoon into 2 well-greased #303 cans. Bake for 35 minutes. Test for doneness with knife blade. Cool in cans for about 10 minutes before slicing. Serve with cream cheese.

MUFFINS

Preheat oven to 400°
1 egg beaten
1 cup milk
¹/₄ cup melted shortening
2 cups sifted whole wheat flour
¹/₄ cup wheat germ
1 tablespoon baking powder
¹/₂ teaspoon salt
¹/₄ cup sugar or molasses
Combine milk and egg. Stir into dry ingredients. Add shortening. Stir lightly. Batter should still have lumps. Fill small greased muffin tins about ³/₄ full. Bake 10–15 minutes. Makes 2 dozen small muffins or 1 dozen regular size.

POPOVERS

Preheat oven to 475°
4 well beaten eggs

2 cups milk
2 tablespoons oil (or melted butter)
2 cups flour
1 teaspoon salt
1 tablespoon sugar

Beat eggs well with egg beater or hand whisk. Add milk and oil; mix well. Sift dry ingredients together and add to liquid mixture. Beat until smooth. Fill well-greased muffin tins ⅓ full. Bake for 15 minutes. Reduce heat immediately to 350° and continue baking for 20–25 minutes. Makes approximately 24 popovers. Serve with butter, honey, jam.

An oven with a glass door provides children with the opportunity to watch the batter rise.

FRENCH TOAST

4 slices bread (cut in half)
2 eggs
¼ cup milk
⅛ teaspoon salt
1 tablespoon sugar
½ teaspoon vanilla
1 tablespoon butter
1 teaspoon grated orange or lemon rind (optional)

Beat eggs, milk, salt, sugar, vanilla, and rind together. Heat butter in frying pan (an electric pan at the table works well). Have egg mixture in a shallow flat dish. Soak bread in mixture and brown on both sides. Serve with syrup or powdered sugar.

PANCAKES

2 cups whole wheat or unbleached white flour
½ teaspoon salt
3 teaspoons baking powder
¼ cup toasted wheat germ
1 tablespoon honey
2 eggs
1¼ cups milk
¼ cup melted shortening

Let children measure and sift together flour, salt, and baking powder. Stir in wheat germ. Beat eggs; stir in milk and honey. Combine with dry ingredients. Mix until smooth, but do not overmix. Add melted shortening. Grease and heat electric frying pan at the table. Drop batter by the spoonful on hot pan (medium high heat). When bubbles appear on the surface the pancake is ready to be turned over. Serve hot with melted butter and syrup or honey.

Suggestions: Let children vary the recipe by selecting other ingredients to add to the batter, such as blueberries, chopped nuts, diced apples, raisins.

This is also a good opportunity to introduce them to different toppings. Suggest they put a dab of sour cream and brown sugar on a bite of pancake, or try fresh fruit with yogurt, or sugar and cinnamon. In this way children learn that certain foods do not always have to be prepared in exactly the same way. They can *experiment with different tastes in small portions and discover the fun of creating their own recipes. Makes 3 dozen small pancakes.*

A good storybook to read before this cooking project is *Pancakes, Pancakes!* by Eric Carle (New York: Alfred A. Knopf, 1970). Bright collage-type illustrations show where the flour, eggs, milk, and butter come from; text explains how to cook pancakes.

Spreads

BUTTER

Whipping cream
Salt
Yellow food coloring
Shake whipping cream in jars or beat with egg beater until butter is formed. Rinse with water and press out excess milk with spoon. Serve sweet or add a little food coloring and salt to taste. Serve with sour dough French bread or soda crackers.

PEANUT BUTTER

2 cups toasted peanuts in the shell
2 tablespoons salad oil
Salt to taste
Let children shell the peanuts allowing enough extra for them to eat. Put peanuts through a grinder or blender. If a hand-style meat grinder is used you may want to put the peanuts through twice. Add oil and salt.

HONEY BUTTER SPREAD

Two parts butter
One part honey
Dash of cinnamon (optional)
Stir until well mixed. Serve with hot biscuits.

Salads

FRUIT SALAD

Invite children and parents to contribute whatever fresh local fruits they can bring to school. In addition, have on hand such fruits as bananas, apples, oranges, fresh pineapple, peaches, pears, mangoes, papayas, seedless grapes, and tangerines.

Whenever possible, try to introduce some less common varieties of fruits along with the familiar ones.

Let children help peel bananas, oranges, wash grapes, and cut the fruit with blunt or serrated knives.

A mixture of plain or flavored yogurt with a tablespoon or two of honey makes a delicious topping, or some children may prefer to eat the fruit salad without topping. Suggestions: Preparation of a "community" fruit salad provides an excellent opportunity for

HELPFUL HINTS

a social occasion among adults as well as children. This should be an unhurried, relaxed project with plenty of time for discussion about colors, contrasts, taste, how different fruits grow. Some of the adults might be responsible for looking up information about the various fruits, how and where they grow, before the salad preparation. Learnings can be reinforced by collecting and posting pictures of the fruit and letting the children identify and talk about them.

In season, use a variety of melons and berries for a colorful and delicious mixture.

AN ACTIVITIES HANDBOOK FOR TEACHERS OF YOUNG CHILDREN

HELPFUL HINTS

1. *Children love to prepare and eat mashed potatoes.*
2. *In selecting a cooking project, list all the possibilities it can provide children for learning concepts through active involvement (washing, scrubbing, peeling, cutting, comparing, learning about shapes, textures, colors.)*
3. *Offer new foods more than once.*
4. *Save pumpkin seeds from your jack o'lantern; soak them in salt water and toast in oven.*

WALDORF SALAD

½ *lb. celery root*
6 medium carrots
2 apples
1 large orange
2 pineapple rings or ¾ *cup pineapple bits*
⅓ *cup raisins*
½ *cup chopped nuts such as walnuts, pecans or almonds (optional)*
Juice of 2 lemons
½ *cup whipping cream*
1 tablespoon honey

Wash and peel celery root and carrots. Shred finely and sprinkle lemon juice over the celery root to prevent darkening. Next shred or dice the apples (peeled or unpeeled). Peel and dice the orange. Add pineapple bits, raisins, and nuts. Whip the cream, fold in honey, and stir into salad mixture.

Suggestions: This is a good opportunity for children to have practice at shredding. Be careful that they do not get their fingers too close to the shredder. Adults should finish the shredding while the children cut the fruit and prepare the dressing. Makes 12–15 small servings.

COTTAGE CHEESE

1 quart milk
2 tablespoons vinegar
Salt
Sour cream (optional)
Fruit

Heat milk until bubbles begin to form (should feel hot to the touch). Remove from heat and stir in vinegar, continuing to stir while mixture cools and curd forms. Hold a strainer over a glass bowl and separate the curds from the liquid (whey). Gently press the curds with a wooden spoon to further squeeze out the whey. Add salt to taste and a little sour cream for smoothness. Serve the curds (cottage cheese) with fresh fruit.

POTATO SALAD

4–6 medium sized boiled potatoes
2 hard boiled eggs
1 can pitted olives
½ *cup mayonnaise*

Salt and pepper to taste

Let children peel and dice the potatoes and eggs. Cut olives into small pieces. Mix all ingredients together.

Suggestions: This is a good recipe for beginners because the ingredients are easy to peel and cut. Serrated knives work well in this project. Children who have never been allowed to cut with knives enjoy the success they have with cutting potatoes. The salad is made fairly quickly and they can taste their results without having to wait.

Other ingredients such as cooked diced ham, tuna, celery, onions, etc. can be added according to the desire of the group. Makes 12–15 small servings.

MACARONI SALAD

2 cups uncooked macaroni for salad
3–4 hard boiled eggs
½ cup celery diced
6 radishes
small bunch of parsley
1½ cups shredded cheddar cheese
½ cup pitted olives
1 cup mayonnaise
Seasoning to taste

Cook and drain macaroni according to directions on package. Let children peel and cut eggs, dice the celery and olives, and shred the cheese. Adults can slice radishes and chop parsley. Mix all ingredients with mayonnaise. Season with salt and pepper to taste. Makes 15–20 small servings.

Eggs

SCRAMBLED EGGS

6 eggs
⅓ cup milk
½ teaspoon salt
2 tablespoons butter

Break eggs into large bowl. Beat with egg beater; add milk and salt. Melt butter in an electric frying pan placed on the table so children can help with the cooking. Set temp. of pan at low so eggs will cook slowly. Pour mixture into the pan and use wooden spoons or spatula to pull cooked egg away from the sides of the pan. Have them stir and move the mixture around so the uncooked portions get cooked. Eat immediately. Makes 10 small servings.

Provide a variety of other ingredients for children to add to their eggs, such as cooked diced ham, shrimp, mushrooms, onions, cheese.

Suggestions: Children who are experienced in cracking eggs can use this occasion to practice separating the yolk from the white since making a "mistake" won't matter.

Discuss other ways eggs are cooked—poaching, baking, boiling, frying sunny-side-up, etc.—and what happens to the whites and yolks. What is an egg? What can it grow into?

HELPFUL HINTS

> 1. *Wash hands before and after a cooking project.*
> 2. *Avoid foods that spoil rapidly. Keep sauces, meats, and dairy products refrigerated.*
> 3. *Keep all cooking utensils clean.*
> 4. *Children and teachers with colds should not help with food preparation.*

DEVILED EGGS

6 hard boiled eggs
3 tablespoons mayonnaise
1 teaspoon prepared mustard
Celery salt
Peel and cut eggs in half lengthwise. Remove yolks and mash with mayonnaise, mustard, and celery salt to taste. Let children stuff the whites with small spoons or forks or with cake decorators. Eggs can be decorated with sprigs of parsley, stuffed olives, or paprika.

EGG FOO YOUNG

4 eggs
½ teaspoon salt
⅓ cup finely cut carrots (raw)
⅓ cup finely cut celery
⅓ cup fresh garden peas
¼ cup diced scallions or green onions
Oil for cooking
Cook carrots, celery, and peas in the smallest amount of water necessary (about ⅓ cup water in a covered pan for about 5 minutes or less). Break eggs into a bowl and beat with an egg beater. Add scallions, salt, and cooked drained vegetables. Pour enough cooking oil into electric fry pan just to coat. Turn heat to medium. Spoon in egg mixture to make small pancake-sized egg foo young. Cook until top is nearly firm. Turn with a spatula and cook on other side for another minute or two. Makes 16 small pancakes.

    Suggestions: *This recipe can be varied to suit the needs of the teacher and children. Cooked diced ham, chicken, pork, shrimp, crabmeat, etc. can be added; bean sprouts or diced bell peppers can also be substituted sometimes in order to let the children taste new foods.*

Rice

STEAMED RICE

2 cups long grain white or brown rice
3 cups water
Put rice into a large pot and add enough water to cover. Let children stand at the sink and wash the rice by rubbing it between their hands. Rinse the rice several times. Add 3 cups water and cover pan with tight fitting lid. Cook rice on high heat until most of the water is cooked away. Turn heat down as low as pos-

sible and steam the rice for about 25 minutes. Fluff rice with a fork before serving. Children like rice with butter and salt or cinnamon and brown sugar. Makes 20 servings.

FRIED RICE

4 cups cooked rice (leftover day old rice is best)
2 eggs
2 green onions
½ cup cooked meat such as pork, beef, chicken
2–3 tablespoons soy sauce
Scramble two eggs and set aside. Clean and dice green onions, stems and all. Add to diced cooked meat and stir fry meat and onions until heated through. Set aside. Heat two tablespoons oil in frying pan and add cooked rice. Stir and cook until rice is heated through. If rice is very dry, you may need to add a little water and cover the pan in order to thoroughly heat the rice. Add all other ingredients, including soy sauce. Stir until meat, onions, and eggs are evenly distributed. Serve with extra soy sauce. Makes 10–12 servings.

OSUSHI

2 cups short grain rice
2 cups water
Grated carrot, peas, mushrooms (optional)
Wash and cook rice as in steamed rice. Meanwhile make sushi su (vinegar) by boiling together
¼ cup white vinegar
2 tablespoons sugar
½ tablespoon salt
When rice is cooked, pour into a flat pan and spread it out. Pour sushi su over the rice. Cool immediately by fanning. Let children form the rice into balls about the size of an egg. Bits of grated carrot, peas, mushrooms, or other vegetables can be added for color and variety. Makes 24 small servings.

Meat

MEATBALLS

1 lb. ground beef
½ cup bread crumbs
½ cup canned milk
1 egg
(¼ cup wheat germ and powdered milk can be added)
Seasonings to taste
Mix all ingredients together and form into small balls. Cook in a lightly greased electric fry pan at the table, browning meat balls on all sides. Serve plain or with hot noodles and a simple tomato sauce with Italian seasoning. Makes about 2 dozen small meatballs.

PASTIES

1 lb. raw ground turkey (ground chicken, ham, or beef can be substituted; also, cooked, ground-up leftover meats)
1 cup finely chopped onions (combine with a few green onions for color)

½ cup wheat germ (plain or toasted)
3–4 cloves crushed garlic
1 teaspoon salt
½ teaspoon pepper
1 teaspoon oregano
4 packages refrigerator biscuits (8 oz. each)
Grated cheese (sharp cheddar and parmesan work well)
Optional ingredients: grated carrots, chopped eggs, mushrooms, cooked potatoes, chopped parsley.

Mix together first 7 ingredients and stir fry over high to medium heat until cooked through. (Drain off grease if you substitute beef or other fatty meat.) Let cool. Preheat oven to 375°. Prepare plates of cheese and other optional ingredients. Let children roll out or flatten individual biscuits (use a little flour if necessary). Each child can spoon a small amount of meat (about 1 teaspoon) on a biscuit and add cheese, carrots, etc., as desired. Moisten edges of biscuit dough with water and pinch together with fingers or tines of fork into crescent shapes. When ready to bake, place pasties on a lightly greased cookie sheet, brush each one with a mixture of 1 egg beaten with 1 teaspoon water. Perforate with fork. Bake for 10–12 minutes. Cool slightly before eating. Makes 48 small pasties.

TERIYAKI MEATBALLS

1 lb. ground beef
½ cup bread crumbs or cooked rice
½ teaspoon garlic puree
¼ cup soy sauce
¼ teaspoon powdered ginger
¼ cup water
1 tablespoon honey

Mix all ingredients together and form into small balls. Cook in a lightly greased electric skillet at the table, browning meat balls on all sides. Serve with rice and soy sauce. Makes about 2 dozen small meatballs.

MUFFIN PIZZAS

8 English muffins (16 halves)
1 can (15 oz.) tomato sauce
1 teaspoon garlic salt
1 teaspoon Italian seasoning
Mozzarella cheese, ground beef, sausage, salami, onions, olives, green pepper, mushrooms, etc.

Add garlic salt and Italian seasoning to tomato sauce and heat through. Toast muffins lightly. Spread sauce on each half and let children select ingredients they want to use on each pizza. Bake in hot (450°) oven until meat is cooked, or place under broiler for a few minutes.

Vegetables

VEGETABLE SOUP

A variety of vegetables, such as
carrots, potatoes, celery, tomatoes,

onions, peas, beans
Soup stock made with meat bones or instant
  soup base and water[1]
Alphabet noodles or rice (optional)
Seasonings to taste
Plant a garden in the nursery school yard and have the children harvest the vegetables, or invite children to bring vegetables from home. Talk about colors, textures, and tastes while children help to wash, scrape, and peel the vegetables.

Make soup stock in pressure cooker or electric pan. Let children add their vegetables. Add a handful of alphabet noodles or rice if desired. Season with salt, oregano, herbs, etc. to taste.

GLAZED CARROTS

4 carrots
1 tablespoon butter
1 tablespoon brown sugar or honey
¼ cup water
Peel and slice carrots into thin strips. Place in a large electric fry pan. Add mixture of butter, sugar, and water. Cover and cook slowly at the table, stirring occasionally until tender. Makes 6–8 servings.

RAW VEGETABLE PLATTER

Provide a variety of raw vegetables such as: carrots, tomatoes, bell peppers, radishes, celery, cauliflower, cucumbers. Wash and cut into bite size pieces. Arrange attractively on platter at each lunch or juice table.

Suggestions: Introduce new foods such as fresh peeled water chestnuts, Jerusalem artichokes, and jicama.

LATKES (POTATO PANCAKES)

2 medium potatoes
¼ cup flour
1 egg
1 teaspoon salt
Peel and grate the potatoes coarsely. Mix with slightly beaten egg, flour, and salt. Fry tablespoonful-size pancakes in hot vegetable oil. Brown on both sides. Serve with sour cream or applesauce. Makes 10–12 small latkes.

Desserts and Snacks

LACE QUICKIES

Preheat oven to 375°
Sift together into a bowl:
½ cup flour
¼ teaspoon baking powder
½ cup sugar
Stir in ½ cup quick cooking oats. Melt in a pan ⅓ cup butter.

---

[1] Another simple soup base can be made by browning lean hamburger with minced onion and adding tomato sauce, bouillon cubes, and water.

Stir in 2 tablespoons light corn syrup, 1 tablespoon vanilla extract, 2 tablespoons cream or evaporated milk. Pour liquid into dry ingredients. Mix all together and drop by the teaspoonful four inches apart onto ungreased cookie sheet. Bake about 8 minutes. Makes about 2 dozen small cookies.

JACK O'LANTERN TREATS

Save the seeds from jack o' lantern pumpkin. Dip them in a solution of salt water (1 tablespoon diluted in 1½ cups water). Drain and spread the seeds on a cookie sheet and bake in 350° oven. Stir to dry out and toast lightly on all sides. Teach the children how to crack and eat the toasted seeds.

Steam or bake pieces of the pumpkin until tender. Mash the cooked squash and use for cookies:

½ cup butter or margarine (1 stick)
1¼ cups brown sugar
2 eggs
1½ cups cooked mashed pumpkin
½ teaspoon salt
½ teaspoon ginger
½ teaspoon cinnamon
½ teaspoon nutmeg
2¼ cups sifted flour
4 teaspoons baking powder
1 teaspoon vanilla
1 cup raisins
1 cup walnuts (optional)
Cream butter and sugar well. Add eggs, pumpkin, and seasonings. Mix well. Sift flour and baking powder together; stir in raisins and nuts. Add flour mixture slowly to creamed mixture and blend well. Stir in vanilla. Drop teaspoonsful onto greased cookie sheet. Bake in preheated 375° oven about 15 minutes or until lightly browned. Makes about 3 dozen cookies.

PUDDLE CAKE

Preheat oven to 350°
Sift into ungreased 8 × 8 × 2 pan:
1½ cups sifted unbleached white or whole wheat pastry flour
3 tablespoons cocoa (or carob powder)
½ teaspoon salt
1 cup brown sugar
1 teaspoon soda
Make a puddle in center by adding 6 tablespoons salad oil, 1 teaspoon vanilla, and 1 tablespoon vinegar. Pour over top 1 cup cold water. Stir with spoon until smooth. Bake 35–40 minutes. Serves 12–15.

SIMPLE GRAHAM CRACKER DESSERT

Preheat oven to 350°
14 Graham crackers
3 eggs
1 cup brown sugar
1 cup nuts
1 teaspoon baking powder
½ cup dates

> 1. Sit down and eat with the children. Show them how you enjoy food.
> 2. Talk about different kinds of foods.
> 3. Notice if young children are influenced in their eating habits by TV commercials.
> 4. Send notes home about good nutrition and the new foods each child has helped prepare in school.
> 5. Invite parents to share their recipes with the school.

Let children crumble the Graham crackers. Cut dates into small pieces. Mix everything together. Put in greased pan and bake 15 minutes. Raisins and other dried fruit may also be added or substituted. Serves 8–10.

APPLESAUCE

6 tart apples
3–4 tablespoons honey
1¼ cups water
Cinnamon
Let children help peel, core, and slice the apples. Cover and cook in water until tender—approximately 20–30 minutes. Add honey and cinnamon to taste. Makes 12 small servings.

JELLO

1 3 oz. package jello
1 cup boiling water
8–10 ice cubes
Mix Jello in boiling water. Stir in ice cubes. Let children stir and watch Jello thicken.
Pour into small (3 oz.) paper cold drink cups and refrigerate. Children can eat Jello before the end of the nursery school day. Makes 6 servings.
Call attention to other substances that dissolve.

STRAWBERRY YOGURT

1 cup strawberries
⅓ cup powdered milk
1 cup yogurt (plain or strawberry flavored)
Mash strawberries. Beat in powdered milk; add yogurt. Serve in small cups. Bananas or other fresh fruit can be substituted. Makes 6–8 small servings.

BANANA-WHEAT GERM SNACKS

Bananas
Toasted wheat germ
Milk
Honey
Let children peel and cut bananas into bite size pieces. Dip each piece into a mixture of half milk and half honey. Drop pieces of banana into a plastic bag filled with wheat germ and shake until well coated. Serve on a tray with colored tooth-picks.

CRUNCHY SNACKS

3 cups old fashioned oats
1 cup unsweetened coconut
1 cup wheat germ (toasted or untoasted)
½ cup (more or less) chopped blanched almonds
Mix above ingredients in a large bowl. Warm the following ingredients in a small sauce pan:
½ cup honey
2 tablespoons water
¼ cup oil or melted butter
Mix and pour liquids over oat mixture and blend well so all particles are coated. Spread in a thin layer (no more than ½ inch) on cookie sheet and toast for about 20 minutes in 250° oven. Stir occasionally to toast evenly. Serve as a snack.

CHEESE CRISPIES

Preheat oven to 375°
2 cups (about ½ lb.) grated sharp cheddar cheese
½ cup (one stick) butter softened
1 cup sifted flour
¼ teaspoon salt
Let children combine all the ingredients with their hands or with a pastry blender until thoroughly mixed. Form into small balls and place an inch apart on cookie sheet. Bake for about 12 minutes.

POPCORN

Popcorn
Oil
Salt
Melted butter (optional)
Pour about ¼ cup oil into electric popcorn popper (preferably the kind with glass top so children can watch). Add popcorn to cover. Have bowls or baskets handy so children can salt small amounts of popcorn to share.

Suggestions: Let children examine the kernels of corn before popping. Explain that this is a special kind of corn grown just for popping and that it is different from the kind we eat off the cob. Each kernel of popcorn has moisture ("a drop of water") inside of it and when the popcorn gets hot, the moisture turns into steam and causes the popcorn to explode.

Place an electric popper without the top on a large sheet spread on the floor. Have children sit 'way back and watch how far the corn can pop.

Play the record "Popcorn," by Hot Butter (Stereo MS3242—Musicor Records, A Division of Talmadge Productions, Inc., 240 W. 55th St., New York, N.Y. 10019).

COLORED MILK

Add a few drops of vanilla and a teaspoonful of honey to each glass of milk and let children select food coloring of their choice to stir in.

1. *Cut out pictures of healthful foods—fresh fruits, vegetables, dairy products, meat—and post them for the children to see.*
2. *Invite community workers, such as the doctor, nutritionist, and dentist to visit the school and talk about proper diet.*
3. *Plan parent meetings with speakers from the consumer protection agency. Discuss sensible food purchasing and meal planning.*

LEMONADE

Let children pick lemons, squeeze them, and do the measuring and mixing whenever possible. Dissolve ⅓ cup honey in ½ cup hot water. Add juice of 4 lemons, 4 cups cold water, and a tray of ice cubes. Stir with wooden spoon and add food coloring if desired. Serves 6. Squeezing fresh orange juice also provides a good opportunity for the children and teacher to talk about seeds, colors, taste, thickness of skin and its purpose.

EGG NOG

Beat with rotary beater:
4 eggs
⅓ cup honey

¼ teaspoon salt
Then beat in 4 cups cold milk and 1 teaspoon vanilla. Sprinkle with nutmeg if desired. Serves 8–10.

FRUIT SHAKE

Combine in a one quart plastic container:
2 cups cold juice (such as orange, pineapple, or grape)
½ cup powdered milk
1 drop vanilla
Add crushed ice and shake until mixed. Serves 4–6.

Ice Cream

Every child should experience the fun and excitement of making home-made ice cream. The following recipes are for the old-fashioned hand crank freezer.

VANILLA ICE CREAM

3 eggs
2 quarts milk
2 pints whipping cream
3 tablespoon vanilla
Dash of salt

Cream together sugar and eggs thoroughly. Add milk and cream, stirring constantly. Add vanilla and dash of salt. Pour mixture into the freezer can and chill for 30 minutes. The can should not be more than ⅔ full to allow for expansion.

When chilled, place freezer can of ice cream mix in tub of ice cream maker. Put top and crank in place. Alternately add 1 cup of crushed ice and ¼ cup rock salt until ice and salt mixture comes to the lid of the freezer can (approximately 8 lbs. of ice and 1¼ cups of rock salt). Let children take turns turning the crank slowly until the ice cream is so thick that the handle can no longer be turned (about 30–40 minutes). Drain excess water from tub; remove dasher from the can; plug the hole in the can lid. Leave can of ice cream in tub of ice and salt. Cover entire freezer with a towel or some heavy material and allow to chill for 30 minutes or more. Fruit may be added during the last 20 minutes of cranking.

FRESH STRAWBERRY ICE CREAM

2–3 baskets strawberries
3 cups sugar
Juice of 5 lemons
1 quart milk
1 large (13 fluid oz.) can evaporated milk
1 pint whipping cream
Hull and mash the strawberries with sugar. Add juice of lemons and let mixture stand at room temperature for 1 hour. Add milk and cream and pour into ice cream freezer. Follow above instructions.

Bibliography of Resources

Cookbooks

The following books may be especially helpful to the teacher who wishes to adapt recipes using natural foods.

Albright, Nancy. *The rodale cookbook.* Emmaus, Pa.: Rodale, 1973. A comprehensive book of recipes using natural foods. Useful listings of natural food stores in the United States, nutritional content of many foods, a food substitution table (honey for sugar, etc.), cost table (comparing name brands to homemade foods), and a section of cooking hints.

Cavin, Ruth. *1 pinch of sunshine, ½ cup of rain. Natural food recipes for young people.* New York: Atheneum, 1973. Simple recipes for breakfast, lunch, and dinner, such as "luscious mush," "liver bobs," "apricot leather." Too complex for preschoolers, but useful for ideas.

Croft, Karen B. *The good for me cookbook.* Palo Alto, Ca.: 741 Maplewood Place, 1971. A handmade cookbook for children and adult helpers based on health foods. The booklet is the result of the author's interest in young children, health foods, printing, and art work. Many of the hand-printed recipes are accompanied by pen and ink drawings and personal comments.

Davis, Adelle. *Let's cook it right.* New York: Harcourt, Brace, 1947. Simplified basic recipes with suggestions for variations applying the principles of good nutrition. Many useful ideas and worthwhile information about good health.

————. *Let's have healthy children.* New York: Harcourt, Brace & World, 1959. This book discusses prenatal diet and foods for children during the early years. One of the chapters deals sensibly with eating problems of the preschool child.

El Molino Mills. *El Molino best: tested recipes from El Molino kitchens.* Alhambra, Ca.: El Molino Mills, 1953. A collection of recipes contributed by people who have used whole grains, seeds and legumes in cooking. Many unusual as well as common recipes using unrefined products.

Ferreira, Nancy J. *The mother-child cook book.* Menlo Park, Ca.: Pacific Coast Publishers, 1969. A book written by a nursery school teacher for her classes in an observation nursery school. The recipes are organized with the preschool child and his parent in mind. The appendix is useful in locating recipes which do not require cooking, as well as indoor and outdoor recipes. There is also a good discussion on the development of basic cooking skills such as wrapping, rolling, spreading, etc. as related to gross and fine motor skills and coordination.

Fredericks, Carlton, and Herbert Bailey. *Food facts & fallacies. The intelligent person's guide to nutrition and health.* New York: ARC Books, 1971. A discussion of how diet is related to good health. Some topics include mental illness, old age, pregnancy, cancer, alcoholism; one chapter deals sensibly with children's eating habits.

Friedlander, Barbara. *Cookbook for the new age; earth, water, fire, air.* New York: Macmillan, 1972. A vegetarian cookbook with deliciously imaginative recipes, including stuffed grape leaves, blintzes, carrot torte, lentil paté. Includes a glossary of vegetables and herbs with suggestions for their preparation. Artistic photographs of vegetables by Bob Cato.

Getzoff, Carole. *The natural cook's first book.* New York: Dodd, Mead, 1973. This participation cookbook, aimed for the 8- to 12-year-old, encourages seasonal cooking and the use of natural and whole grains. Recipes can be adapted for use with younger children.

Hunter, Beatrice Trum. *The natural food cookbook.* New York: Pyramid, 1961. Over 2,000 recipes using whole grains and natural foods such as nutritional yeast, wheat germ, soy flour, etc. Has a check list of basic natural foods and sources of supply in the U.S. None of the recipes use baking powder, soda, or white sugar.

Shambala Publications, Inc. *Tassajara bread book.* Berkeley, 1970. A very well-designed booklet written by the Chief Priest of the Zen Center in San Francisco. The recipes are prepared with whole grains with sections devoted to yeasted and unyeasted breads, quick breads, and some interesting background information about Tassajara, the Zen monastery in the hills of Monterey County, California where the students of Zen meditate and exist on a simple diet of vegetables and grains.

Toms, Agnes. *Eat, drink and be healthy.* New York: Pyramid, 1963. A useful book with over 2,000 recipes using natural foods. Salads and desserts are particularly good for use with young children.

Complete List of Activities and Resources

part 1 opportunities for growth in language abilities

part 2   experiences in science

part 3   exploring the arts

part 4 pre-math experiences

part 5 cooking

Photo Credits

DEFGHIJ-M-7987